Coursebook

Margaret O'Keeffe
Lewis Lansford
Ed Pegg

A1 > Business Partner

Contents

UNIT 1 › WELCOME p.7
Videos: 1.1 What's your name? 1.4 Welcoming a visitor

1.1 › Nice to meet you
- **Video:** What's your name?
- **Vocabulary:** Countries and nationalities
- **Communicative grammar:** Introductions
- **Task:** Meeting others and making introductions

1.2 › Can you fill this in, please?
- **Vocabulary:** Personal details
- **Pronunciation:** The alphabet (p.96)
- **Reading and listening:** Filling in forms
- **Grammar:** my, your, his, her, its, our, their
- **Speaking:** Completing a new employee registration form

1.3 › My company
- **Listening and reading:** Buildings, departments and facilities
- **Communicative grammar:** Describing your company
- **Pronunciation:** Plural -s (p.96)
- **Writing:** A description of a company or workplace

1.4 › Work skills: Welcoming a visitor
- **Video:** Welcoming a visitor
- **Speaking:** Workplace visits

1.5 › Business workshop: Your first day
- **Speaking:** Meeting human resources and other team members
- **Writing:** Completing your employee profile

Review p.87

UNIT 2 › WORK p.17
Videos: 2.1 I work in Sales 2.4 Small talk at work

2.1 › What do you do?
- **Video:** I work in Sales
- **Vocabulary:** The work we do
- **Communicative grammar:** Talking about work
- **Task:** Where I work and what I do

2.2 › What does the company do?
- **Vocabulary:** What companies do
- **Pronunciation:** Numbers (p.97)
- **Reading and listening:** Company information
- **Grammar:** a/an
- **Writing:** Describing a company

2.3 › A week in the life
- **Reading:** Two different routines
- **Communicative grammar:** Talking about routines
- **Pronunciation:** Questions (p.97)
- **Writing:** A short blog post for a company intranet

2.4 › Work skills: Small talk
- **Video:** Small talk at work
- **Grammar:** Using 's and s'
- **Speaking:** Making conversation

2.5 › Business workshop: At a conference
- **Reading:** A conference website
- **Listening:** Small talk at a conference
- **Speaking:** Networking

Review p.88

UNIT 3 › WHAT? WHEN? WHERE? p.27
Videos: 3.1 I can work flexible hours 3.4 A progress meeting

3.1 › We're very busy in December
- **Video:** I can work flexible hours
- **Vocabulary:** Months and seasons
- **Communicative grammar:** Talking about ability and possibility; at, in, on, from ... to ...
- **Pronunciation:** can and can't (p.98)
- **Task:** Asking and talking about your partner's work

3.2 › Requests
- **Vocabulary:** Ordinal numbers and dates
- **Pronunciation:** Ordinal numbers (p.98)
- **Reading and listening:** Can I have some time off?
- **Grammar:** Can ... ?/ Could ... ?
- **Speaking:** Talking about taking time off

3.3 › I am writing to complain ...
- **Reading:** Complaints
- **Communicative grammar:** Talking about the past
- **Writing:** An email to describe a problem and request action

3.4 › Work skills: We have a problem
- **Video:** A progress meeting
- **Speaking:** A progress meeting

3.5 › Business workshop: A problem with a client
- **Reading:** A customer complaint
- **Speaking:** A problem-solving meeting; A phone call

Review p.89

UNIT 4 › PROBLEMS AND SOLUTIONS p.37
Videos: 4.1 Problems at work 4.4 There is a problem with ...

4.1 › What went wrong?
- **Video:** Problems at work
- **Vocabulary:** Past irregular verbs
- **Communicative grammar:** Talking about the past: Past Simple
- **Pronunciation:** The -ed ending (p.99)
- **Task:** Talking about problems in the past and how you solved them

4.2 › How can I help?
- **Vocabulary:** Solutions
- **Listening:** On the phone
- **Grammar:** Making offers and promises with will
- **Speaking and writing:** Making phone calls at work

4.3 › We are sorry that ...
- **Reading:** An email of complaint and a reply
- **Communicative grammar:** Using negatives in the past; Asking questions about the past
- **Pronunciation:** 'th' as /θ/ and /ð/ (p.99)
- **Writing:** A reply email

4.4 › Work skills: Face-to-face complaints
- **Video:** There is a problem with ...
- **Speaking:** Responding to a complaint

4.5 › Business workshop: Can I help you?
- **Speaking:** Making phone calls
- **Reading:** An email of complaint
- **Writing:** Replying to a complaint

Review p.90

UNIT 5 › OFFICE DAY TO DAY p.47

Videos: 5.1 What are they doing?   5.4 Can you help me?

5.1 › What are you working on?	5.2 › Are you free at two?	5.3 › Can we meet to discuss … ?	5.4 › Work skills: Can I ask a favour?	5.5 › Business workshop: The meeting is at 3 p.m.
Video: ▶ What are they doing? **Vocabulary:** Word pairs **Communicative grammar:** Talking about things happening now **Pronunciation:** ➜ /ŋ/ and the Present Continuous (p.100) **Task:** Writing about what people are doing now	**Vocabulary:** Word pairs **Listening:** Organising meetings **Speaking:** Arranging and postponing meetings	**Reading:** Emails arranging, accepting or changing a meeting **Communicative grammar:** Talking about future arrangements **Pronunciation:** ➜ /ɪ/ and /iː/ (p.100) **Writing:** An email arranging a meeting	**Video:** ▶ Can you help me? **Speaking:** Doing favours	**Writing:** An email to arrange a meeting to discuss a problem **Speaking:** Postponing a meeting

Review p.91

UNIT 6 › AN OFFICE MOVE p.57

Videos: 6.1 An office move   6.4 A presentation about office equipment

6.1 › It's cheaper and better	6.2 › Which is better?	6.3 › Which is the best?	6.4 › Work skills: As you can see on the slide, …	6.5 › Business workshop: The office move
Video: ▶ An office move **Vocabulary:** Descriptions **Communicative grammar:** Comparing two things **Pronunciation:** ➜ The vowel /ə/ (p.101) **Task:** Choosing a warehouse	**Vocabulary:** Orders **Speaking and reading:** Supplier quotes **Grammar:** 🔗 *good – better – best/bad – worse – worst* **Writing:** Describing different options	**Reading:** An email about changing a mobile phone contract **Communicative grammar:** Making proposals with *if* **Pronunciation:** ➜ /æ/ and /ʌ/ (p.101) **Writing:** An email comparing two offers	**Video:** ▶ A presentation about office equipment **Speaking:** Talking about presentation slides	**Reading:** An email from the boss **Writing and speaking:** Comparing two offices **Speaking:** Presenting your choice

Review p.92

UNIT 7 › PROCEDURES p.67

Videos: 7.1 Paying suppliers   7.4 A new workflow

7.1 › What's the procedure?	7.2 › Workflow	7.3 › A manual	7.4 › Work skills: Changing a workflow	7.5 › Business workshop: How can we improve it?
Video: ▶ Paying suppliers **Vocabulary:** Describing a procedure **Communicative grammar:** Talking about obligation **Task:** Explaining a procedure	**Vocabulary:** Descriptions **Reading and listening:** A workflow problem **Pronunciation:** ➜ /aɪ/ and /eɪ/ (p.102) **Speaking:** Improving a workflow	**Reading:** A manual **Communicative grammar:** Instructions **Pronunciation:** ➜ /l/ and /r/ (p.102) **Writing:** Instructions for creating an invoice	**Video:** ▶ A new workflow **Speaking:** Making and responding to suggestions	**Reading:** Identifying problems in a workflow **Speaking:** Discussing solutions; Responsibilities in a new workflow

Review p.93

UNIT 8 › MANAGING PROJECTS p.77

Videos: 8.1 Making cars at The Morgan Motor Company   8.4 Feedback in the office

8.1 › How long does it take?	8.2 › Reducing costs	8.3 › Planning projects	8.4 › Work skills: Giving feedback	8.5 › Business workshop: Updates and feedback
Video: ▶ Making cars at The Morgan Motor Company **Vocabulary:** Production **Communicative grammar:** Revision of the present **Task:** Explaining information on a database	**Vocabulary:** Saving money **Reading:** An online interview **Communicative grammar:** Revision of the past **Pronunciation:** ➜ Pronouncing the letter 'o' (p.103) **Writing:** Actions and results	**Reading:** Scope statements **Communicative grammar:** Revision of the future **Pronunciation:** ➜ The vowel /ɜː/ (p.103) **Writing:** Scope statements	**Video:** ▶ Feedback in the office **Speaking:** Giving feedback	**Reading:** A team update email **Writing:** Replying to an update **Speaking:** Giving feedback

Review p.94

| Pronunciation p.95 | Irregular verb list p.104 | Grammar reference p.105 | Numbers p.112 | Additional material p.113 | Videoscripts p.123 | Audioscripts p.126 | Vocabulary list p.130 |

Introduction

Who ... is Business Partner for?

- *Business Partner* A1 & A2 is for learners who have studied English before, at school or privately, but what they learnt has not been very useful for them in their job, or they simply don't remember much of it.
- Now they need to study business English in order to better communicate in a workplace that is increasingly international.
- To achieve this, they need to improve their knowledge of the English language but also develop key work skills.
- They need a course which is relevant to their professional needs.

Why ... a communicative methodology?

Students of *Business Partner* may be working in different industries, in different job positions and in different countries but they all have in common the need to communicate in English in an international workplace, in an effective manner.

The objective of the course is to equip students with the skills they need to use English effectively, without anxiety about their language ability.

Why ... work skills training?

Business Partner focuses on delivering practical language and skills training that learners need for successful communication when working with people from different countries, even if those learners begin the course with limited language ability.

In *Business Partner*, every unit has a video-based lesson on 'Work skills' to expose students to best-practice scenarios of various business situations that they can use as models.

The objective of this training is to give learners a better chance of getting a job, or of moving jobs in an organisation.

What's in each unit?

Each unit is divided into five lessons and each lesson starts with a Lesson outcome and ends with a short Self-assessment section: this is to help learners think about the progress that they have made.

Vocabulary and functional language

In order to meet the course objectives, the vocabulary and functional phrases in each unit focus on industries, jobs and job environments that are relevant to students to help them function in a variety of professional situations.

This vocabulary has been selected to answer learners' needs at work and may seem high level or technical compared to a general English course. It is, however, basic professional vocabulary that learners need to function in their jobs.

Grammar

Similarly, the approach to grammar is to help students acquire language to survive in these situations. The grammar content comes from the communicative needs of learners and is given in chunks, with a light approach to rules. The grammar reference section at the back of the book provides additional practice of grammar points and a recorded list of irregular verbs.

Listening and video

There are many listening activities to help develop comprehension skills and to hear language in context. All of the video and audio material is available in MyEnglishLab and includes a range of British, U.S. and non-native-speaker English, so that learners are exposed to a variety of accents, to reflect the reality of their working lives.

Learners will be able to watch and understand short authentic videos, which in turn they can use as a model for the group tasks.

Speaking

There are plenty of opportunities for speaking practice in relevant and engaging activities in each lesson. The objective is to make apprehensive students feel comfortable developing this essential skill for the workplace.

Writing
Learners at this level need to respond to emails and other functional pieces of writing. The lesssons provide a model for students to follow, grammar practice of the structures they need to use when writing and functional language stems to help them. The writing tasks allow freer practice of the target vocabulary and grammar, and offer elements of personalisation where possible.

Work skills
Through authentic videos, students are shown best-practice scenarios of different work situations. They then have the chance to study and practise the relevant functional language from each situation. Finally, students are encouraged to activate the skills and language they have learnt and practised by collaborating on group tasks.

Business workshops
Business workshops allow learners to focus mostly on speaking and writing, and offer a practical application and review of the content of the unit.

Pronunciation
Two pronunciation points are presented and practised in every unit, which are linked to the content of the units. The Pronunciation bank is at the back of the book with signposts from the relevant lessons. This section also includes a phonetic chart for British English and American English.

Reviews
There is a one-page review for each unit at the back of the coursebook. The review recycles and revises the key vocabulary, grammar and functional language presented in the unit.

Signposts, cross-references and the Pearson English Portal

Signposts for teachers 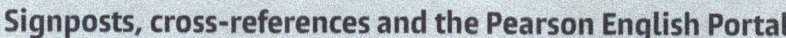 in each lesson indicate that there are extra activities in the Portal which can be printed or displayed on-screen. These activities can be used to extend a lesson or to focus in more depth on a particular section.

 page 000

Cross-references refer to the Pronunciation bank and Grammar reference pages.

PearsonEnglishPortal

Access to the Pearson English Portal is given through a code printed on the inside front cover of this book.

The code will give you access to:

Interactive eBook: a digital version of the coursebook including interactive activities, all class video clips and all class audio recordings.

Online Practice on MyEnglishLab: a self-study interactive workbook with instant feedback and automatic gradebook. Teachers can assign workbook activities as homework.

Digital Resources: including downloadable coursebook resources, all video clips, all audio recordings.

The **Global Scale of English (GSE)** is a standardised, granular scale from 10 to 90 which measures English language proficiency. The GSE Learning Objectives for Professional English are aligned with the Common European Framework of Reference (CEFR). Unlike the CEFR, which describes proficiency in terms of broad levels, the Global Scale of English identifies what a learner can do at each point on a more granular scale – and within a CEFR level. The scale is designed to motivate learners by demonstrating incremental progress in their language ability. The Global Scale of English forms the backbone for Pearson English course material and assessment.

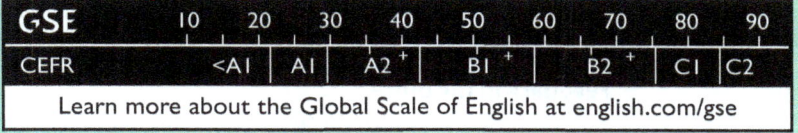

Learn more about the Global Scale of English at english.com/gse

COMMUNICATION SKILLS
Video introduction

Introduction The Work skills videos (in Lesson 4 of each unit) show people in situations at work.

Murray&Jahner is an international consumer goods company. They sell many products to the market and work with top brands. Yumiko Kobayashi is the Director at the London office. In the videos we see her and other employees at work: in meetings, presentations and day-to-day interactions.

Characters

Yumiko Kobayashi, Japanese
(units 1, 3, 5, 6, 7, 8)

Krzysztof Grzeszak, Polish
(units 1, 6)

Liz Rendell, American
(units 1, 4)

Andrea Hofmann, German
(units 2, 5, 8)

Jack Taylor, British
(units 2, 5)

Martin Evans, British
(units 3, 5, 6)

Emily Davies, British
(unit 4)

Paulo Caruso, Brazilian-British
(units 3, 5, 7)

Rachel Peters, British
(units 3, 5, 8)

Video summary

1. **Welcoming a visitor**
   Unit 1 video: *Krzysztof arrives for a meeting with Yumiko in the office.*

2. **Small talk at work**
   Unit 2 video: *Andrea meets Jack, a new employee.*

3. **A progress meeting**
   Unit 3 video: *Yumiko asks for an update from her team.*

4. **There is a problem with …**
   Unit 4 video: *Liz shows her broken phone to a Customer Service Assistant.*

5. **Can you help me?**
   Unit 5 video: *Employees ask for and offer help.*

6. **A presentation about office equipment**
   Unit 6 video: *Krzysztof gives a presentation about printers to Yumiko and Martin.*

7. **A new workflow**
   Unit 7 video: *Yumiko and Paulo talk about how to improve the onboarding process for new employees.*

8. **Feedback in the office**
   Unit 8 video: *Yumiko gives feedback to Andrea and Rachel on their work.*

Welcome 1

Unit overview

1.1	**Nice to meet you** **Lesson outcome:** Learners can introduce themselves and others and say where they are from.	**Vocabulary:** Countries and nationalities **Communicative grammar:** Introductions **Video:** What's your name? **Task:** Meeting others and making introductions
1.2	**Can you fill this in, please?** **Lesson outcome:** Learners can complete a form giving personal details about themselves.	**Vocabulary:** Personal details **Reading and listening:** Filling in forms **Speaking:** Completing a new employee registration form
1.3	**My company** **Lesson outcome:** Learners can describe their company and workplace.	**Listening and reading:** Buildings, departments and facilities **Communicative grammar:** Describing your company **Writing:** A description of a company or workplace
1.4	**Work skills:** Welcoming a visitor **Lesson outcome:** Learners can introduce themselves when visiting a company, greet visitors to their place of work and make simple offers.	**Video:** Welcoming a visitor **Speaking:** Workplace visits
1.5	**Business workshop:** Your first day **Lesson outcome:** Learners can introduce themselves in a new job for the first time, meet new colleagues and complete an employee profile.	**Speaking:** Meeting human resources and other team members **Writing:** Completing your employee profile

Review 1: p.87 | **Pronunciation:** 1.2 The alphabet 1.3 Plural -s p.96 | **Grammar reference:** 1.1 Introductions 1.2 *my, your, his, her, its, our, their* 1.3 Describing your company p.105

1.1 Nice to meet you

Lesson outcome Learners can introduce themselves and others and say where they are from.

Lead-in **1A** 🔊 1.01 Listen and match 1–3 with a–c.

1 Lena, this is Jorge. a I'm Irish.
2 I'm Kathy. b Are you Miss Sato?
3 Excuse me. c He's from Spain.

B 🔊 1.02 Complete the dialogues with the sentences in Exercise 1A. Then listen and check.

Nice to meet you.
A _____

Yes, I am.
B _____

Hi. I'm Lena. I'm from Germany.
C _1c_

Vocabulary Countries and nationalities

2 Match the flags with the countries in the box.

Brazil   India   Japan   Mexico   ~~Poland~~

1 _Poland_   2 _____   3 _____   4 _____   5 _____

3A Choose the correct word.

1 Miguel is *Mexico* / *Mexican*.
2 Marcin is from *Poland* / *Polish*.
3 Paola is *Brazil* / *Brazilian*.
4 Suresh is from *India* / *Indian*.
5 Shoko is *Japan* / *Japanese*.

B 🔊 1.03 Complete the dialogues. Use the countries and nationalities in Exercise 3A. Then listen and check.

1 **Miguel:** Marcin, this **is** Paola. She**'s** ¹_Brazilian_ .
   Marcin: Hi, Paola. Nice to meet you.
   Paola: Nice to meet you, too. Where **are** you from, Marcin?
   Marcin: I**'m** ²_____ .
   Paola: Are you from Warsaw?
   Marcin: No, I**'m not**. I**'m** from Krakow.
   Paola: And **are** you from ³_____ , Miguel?
   Miguel: Yes, that**'s** right.

2 **Suresh:** **Are** you ⁴_____ , Shoko?
   Shoko: Yes, I **am**. I**'m** from Tokyo. And you?
   Suresh: I**'m** from ⁵_____ .
   Shoko: And where **is** Paola from?
   Suresh: She**'s** from ⁶_____ .

4 🔊 1.04 Complete the tables. Then listen and check.

Countries	Nationalities	Countries	Nationalities
Argentina	Argentinian	⁵_____	Japanese
¹_Brazil_	Brazilian	⁶_____	Mexican
China	Chinese	Poland	⁷_____
²_____	German	⁸_____	Spanish
India	³_____	the UK	British
Ireland	⁴_____	the USA	American

Teacher's resources: extra activities

1.1 Nice to meet you

Communicative grammar

> **INTRODUCTIONS** → Grammar reference: page 105

I'm (= I **am**) from Poland.	**I'm not** (= I **am not**) from Poland.
You/We/They**'re** (= You/We/They **are**) from Brazil.	You/We/They **aren't** (= You/We/They **are not**) from Brazil.
He/She/It**'s** (= He/She/It **is**) from Spain.	He/She/It **isn't** (= He/She/It **is not**) from Spain.
Are you/they from Poland? Yes, I **am**. / Yes, they **are**. No, I**'m not** (= I **am not**). / No, they **aren't** (= they **are not**).	**Is** he/she/it from Poland? Yes, he/she/it **is**. No, he/she/it **isn't** (= he/she/it **is not**).
What**'s** (= What **is**) your name? Where **are** you from?	**I'm** (= I **am**) Kathy. My name**'s** (= My name **is**) Mark. This **is** Julia.

```
'm    'm not    are (x4)
aren't    is    isn't    's
```

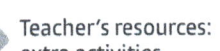
Teacher's resources: extra activities

5 🔊 1.05 Complete the dialogue with the words in the box. Then listen and check.

Hans: Hello, I ¹___'m___ Hans.
Maria: Hi, Hans. My name ²_____ Maria.
Hans: Nice to meet you.
Maria: Nice to meet you, too.
Hans: ³_____ you from Argentina?
Maria: No, I ⁴_____ . I'm Brazilian.
Hans: Is your boss Brazilian?
Maria: No, she ⁵_____ . She's from Mexico.
Mike: Maria! Hello!
Maria: Hi, Mike! And Lisa! Hans, this ⁶_____ Mike and Lisa. They ⁷_____ from the UK.
Hans: Nice to meet you.
Mike: Nice to meet you, Hans.
Lisa: Hi.
Hans: ⁸_____ you from London?
Lisa: No, we ⁹_____ . We ¹⁰_____ from Liverpool.

VIDEO

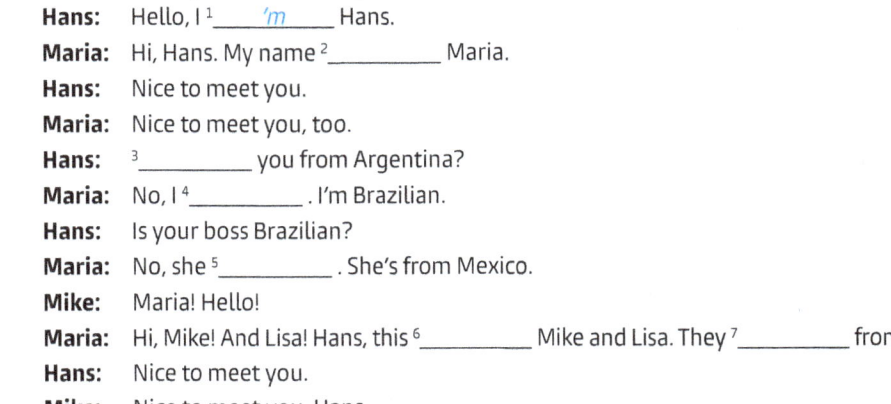

6 ▶ 1.1.1 Watch the video and answer the questions.
1 Watch Part 1. Are the sentences *true* (T) or *false* (F)?
   a Her name is Asako.   b She is Japanese.   c She's a Designer.
2 Watch Part 2. Answer the questions.
   a Are they German?   b Are they from Warsaw?   c Is she an Office Manager?
3 Watch Part 3. Answer the questions.
   a What's his name?   b Where is he from?   c What's his nationality?

TASK

7A Work in pairs. Take turns meeting each other and introducing yourselves. Talk about your name, nationality and job.
A: *Hi. My name's Luis. I'm Spanish.*
B: *Hi, Luis. I'm Lise.*
A: *Where are you from?*
B: *I'm German. I'm from Berlin. Where are you from?*
A: *I'm from Spain – from Madrid.*

B Now work with another pair. Take turns introducing yourself and your partner. Ask questions.

C Put the words in the correct order. Say goodbye to each other.

```
you    later    see
```

Self-assessment I can introduce myself and others and say where we are from.

1.2 Can you fill this in, please?

Lesson outcome — Learners can complete a form giving personal details about themselves.

Lead-in

1 🔊 1.06 Look at the employee identification card. Complete the dialogue with the words in the box. There is one extra word. Then listen and check.

| address | email address | ID card number | passport | phone number |

EMPLOYEE IDENTIFICATION
Jacek Iwaniec
j.iwaniec@ccce.com
Carlton Carbon Consulting & Engineering
28 Oak Road, London W55 1TF
Tel 020 7946 0800
ID NUMBER 124232

Leah: What's your ^{1}_____, Jacek?
Jacek: It's 28 Oak Road, London, W55 1TF.
Leah: What's your ^{2}_____?
Jacek: It's 124232.
Leah: What's your ^{3}_____?
Jacek: It's j.iwaniec@ccce.com. All lower case.
Leah: OK, thanks. And what's your ^{4}_____?
Jacek: It's 020 7946 0800.

Vocabulary — Personal details

2 Look at the hotel guest information. Match 1–9 with a–i.

a first name / given name __2__
b surname / last name ____
c title ____
d nationality ____
e middle name ____
f postcode / zip code ____
g home address ____
h passport / ID card number ____
i phone/mobile/cell number _____

HOTEL IQBAL: GUEST INFORMATION
^{1}Mr ^{2}Wilhelm ^{3}Ernst ^{4}Schmidt
^{5}Chausseestrasse 41
Teterow, Germany
^{6}17161
T: ^{7}03996 55 06 78
E: W_Schmidt@net-mail.com
^{8}German
^{9}Identification card number T29445678
One room, two nights
Leisure/Business

3 Write information about yourself.

HOTEL ARKADIA: GUEST INFORMATION

TITLE: MR / MS / OTHER _____ FIRST NAME _____
MIDDLE NAME _____ SURNAME _____
HOME ADDRESS _____
POSTCODE _____
EMAIL ADDRESS _____ MOBILE NUMBER _____
NATIONALITY _____ PASSPORT / ID CARD NUMBER _____
ARRIVAL DATE _____ ARRIVAL TIME _____

➡ **page 96** See Pronunciation bank: The alphabet

4A Match 1–7 with a–g.
a dot ____   c hyphen ____   e lower case *n* ____   g all lower case ____
b at ____   d underscore ____   f capital *W* ____

B 🔊 1.07 Listen and practise saying the email address in Exercise 4A.

C 🔊 1.08 Listen and write the email addresses.
1 ___ben@abc.net___   4 _____
2 _____   5 _____
3 _____

D Practise saying email addresses. Ask your classmates.
What's your email address?
It's jorge underscore gomez at net hyphen mail dot com. It's all lower case.

1.2 Can you fill this in, please?

Reading and listening

Filling in forms

5A 🔊 1.09 Look at the new employee registration form. Then listen to Anna's phone conversation and complete the form.

NEW EMPLOYEE REGISTRATION

Surname ¹ _____ Weber _____
First name ² _____ Anna _____
Gender: ³ male ☐   female ☐   other ☐
Nationality ⁴ _____
Marital status: ⁵ single ☐   married ☐   other ☐
Email address ⁶ _____
Phone / mobile / cell number ⁷ _____
Emergency contact number ⁸ _____
ID card / Passport number ⁹ _____
Healthcard #

Phone numbers			
0	00	22	653-3340
oh	double oh	double two	six five three, double-three four oh
zero	zero zero	two two	six five three, three three four zero

➡ **page 112** See Numbers

B Match 1–6 with a–f. Then listen again and check.

1 What's   a nationality?
2 Can you   b your surname?
3 What's your   c that, please?
4 Sorry, could you repeat   d spell that, please?
5 Are you married   e address?
6 What's your email   f or single?

> **MY, YOUR, HIS, HER, ITS, OUR, THEIR**   ➡ Grammar reference: page 105
>
> She's **my** manager.   **Its** name is the Hotel Arkadia.
> What's **your** email address?   **Our** phone number is 232 4578.
> This is **his** office.   What are **your** passport numbers?
> What's **her** nationality?   What's **their** address?

Teacher's resources: extra activities

Speaking

6A Look at the new employee registration form. What questions do you need to ask to get the information? Use Exercise 5B to help you.

New Employee Registration

SURNAME _____   FIRST NAME _____
GENDER: MALE ☐ FEMALE ☐ OTHER ☐   NATIONALITY _____
MARITAL STATUS: SINGLE ☐ MARRIED ☐ OTHER ☐   EMAIL ADDRESS _____
PHONE / MOBILE / CELL NUMBER _____   EMERGENCY CONTACT NUMBER _____
ID CARD OR PASSPORT NUMBER _____
NATIONAL INSURANCE NUMBER

B Work in pairs. Ask and answer the questions. Complete the form with your partner's information.

Self-assessment I can complete a form giving personal details about myself.

1.3 My company

Lesson outcome — Learners can describe their company and workplace.

Lead-in **1** Is your workplace like one of these? Which of these places are in your town or city?
Fashion HiQ has workplaces around the world.

A warehouse, Poland

B office, Germany

C factory, China

Listening **2** 🔊 1.10 Listen to three people who work for the clothing maker Fashion HiQ. Match each speaker with a picture in Exercise 1.
1 ____   2 ____   3 ____

3 Listen again. Tick (✓) the buildings, departments and facilities for each location.

	Buildings			Departments			Facilities		
	factory	office	warehouse	production	sales	shipping and receiving	canteen	gym	employee break room
Head office, Germany		✓							
Manufacturing division, China									
Distribution division, Poland									

4A Look at these staff comments on their workplace. Which comments are positive? Which are negative?

1 The office is **large**.   (+)/ –
2 It's very **light**.   + / –
3 The canteen is **small**.   + / –
4 The factory is **modern**.   + / –
5 It's **noisy**.   + / –
6 The break room is **quiet**.   + / –
7 The warehouse is **old-fashioned** and **dark**.   + / –

B Match 1–4 with a–d.

1 dark   a large
2 noisy   b light
3 old-fashioned   c modern
4 small   d quiet

C Which words in Exercise 4B describe your workplace or place of study?

Reading **5** Complete the description of Fashion HiQ. Use the table in Exercise 3 to help you.

canteen   department   division   factory   gym   manager   office   warehouse

My company has three locations in three countries. **There's** a(n) ¹_____ in Germany, a(n) ²_____ in China and a(n) ³_____ in Poland. I'm a(n) ⁴_____, in the production ⁵_____. It's part of the manufacturing ⁶_____. The factory is modern. At the factory, **there's** a(n) ⁷_____, but **there's no** ⁸_____.

12

1.3 My company

Communicative grammar

> **DESCRIBING YOUR COMPANY** → Grammar reference: page 105
>
> **There's** (= **There is**) a canteen.
> **There's no** gym.
>
> **There are** three departments.
> **There are** small restaurants near the office.
> **There are no** offices.

6 Look at the company information. Are the sentences *true* (T) or *false* (F)?

a/one restaurant → two restaurant**s**
a/one factory → two factor**ies**

Company name: Scarpe, Portafogli e Borse, K.K.		
Head office: Yokohama, Japan	**Factory: Katowice, Poland**	**Warehouse: Naples, Italy**
• sales division • marketing department • Sales Manager, Marketing Manager • gym and canteen	• manufacturing division • production department • Production Manager • canteen	• distribution division • shipping department • Warehouse Manager, Shipping Manager • canteen

1 There's a factory in Naples. *F*
2 There are two managers in the warehouse.
3 There's no gym in Yokohama.
4 There are no factories in Poland.
5 There's a canteen in the warehouse.
6 There's a production department in Katowice.

7 Choose the correct word.

1 There*'s* / *are* four divisions.
2 There*'s* / *are* no warehouses.
3 There*'s* / *are* a factory.
4 There*'s* / *are* break rooms for employees.
5 There*'s* / *are* no canteen.
6 There*'s* / *are* a gym.

8 Complete the sentences with *There's* or *There are*.

1 _____ a sales department in Madrid.
2 _____ large factories in Japan.
3 _____ a canteen in the factory.
4 _____ no managers in the warehouse.
5 _____ three departments in the manufacturing division.
6 _____ no gym for employees.

→ **page 96** See Pronunciation bank: Plural -*s*

T Teacher's resources: extra activities

Writing

9 Write a description of a company and workplace like the one in Exercise 5. Use your own, or the one below. Include information about:
- locations (offices, factories, warehouses, etc., and countries and/or cities).
- departments and/or divisions.
- facilities in the location where you work.

Company name: Muebles Madali, S.A.		
Head office: Madrid, Spain	**Factory: Puebla, Mexico**	**Warehouse: Alicante, Spain**
• sales division • marketing department • example job: Sales Rep • offices – light • canteen and gym	• manufacturing division • production department • example job: Engineer • workplace – noisy • restaurants near the factory	• distribution division • shipping department • example job: Warehouse Manager • building – modern • canteen

Self-assessment

I can describe my company and workplace.

1.4 WORK SKILLS
Welcoming a visitor

Lesson outcome Learners can introduce themselves when visiting a company, greet visitors to their place of work and make simple offers.

Lead-in 1A Match the photos (A and B) with the situations in the box. There is one extra situation.

saying hello to a friendly visitor   introducing a colleague   giving your name at reception

B Complete the dialogues in Exercise 1A with sentences a–d.
a Could you spell that, please?
b No, thanks.
c My name's Krzysztof Grzeszak.
d Good to see you! How about a coffee?

VIDEO 2A ▶ 1.4.1 Watch Part 1 of the video without sound. Tick (✓) who says each line.

		Liz	Krzysztof
1	'Good morning. How may I help you?'		
2	'I'm here to see Yumiko Kobayashi.'		
3	'Sorry, could you repeat that, please?'		
4	'Have a seat, please.'		
5	'Would you like some tea or coffee?'		
6	'Milk, please. No sugar, thanks.'		

B Watch Part 1 of the video with sound. Check your answers.

3A ▶ 1.4.2 Watch Part 2 of the video. Which of these items are in the video?

tablet

photocopier

laptop

coffee machine

whiteboard

printer

B Is the receptionist and Krzysztof's conversation formal or less formal? And Yumiko and Krzysztof's conversation?

4 Watch the video again. Match 1–5 with a–e and 6–10 with f–j.
1 Could you   a a seat, please.   6 How about   f really well, thanks.
2 Have   b keep you waiting.   7 How   g a coffee?
3 Ms Kobayashi will c repeat that, please?   8 I'm   h you.
4 Sorry to   d see you again!   9 Please   i come in.
5 Good to   e be ready in a few minutes. 10 After   j are you?

1.4 | Work skills: Welcoming a client

Speaking

> **WORKPLACE VISITS**
>
> **Formal language**
>
> **Greetings**
>
> | | |
> |---|---|
> | Good morning. How may I help you? | I'm here to see Mr Lee. My name's Ella Jones. |
> | I'm sorry, he's not at his desk. | |
>
> **Exchanging information**
>
> | | |
> |---|---|
> | What's your name, please? | It's Michael Connery. |
> | Could you repeat that, please? | Yes, it's Michael Connery. |
> | Could you spell that, please? | Sure. M-I-C-H-A- ... |
>
> **Offers**
>
> | | |
> |---|---|
> | Have a seat, please. | Thank you. |
> | Would you like some tea or coffee? | Coffee, please. Thanks. |
> | Would you like milk or sugar? | Milk, please. No sugar, thanks. |
>
> **Less formal language**
>
> **Greetings**
>
> | | |
> |---|---|
> | Hello! Good to see you again! | Good to see you, too! |
> | How are you? | I'm really well, thanks. How about you? |
>
> **Offers**
>
> | | |
> |---|---|
> | How about a coffee / a tea / some water? | No, thanks. / Yes, please. |
> | Please come in. | OK, thanks. |
> | After you. | Thanks. |

T Teacher's resources: extra activities

5 Work in groups of three. Write two dialogues.
Student A: You work at reception.
Student B: You visit Student C.
Student C: Student B visits you.

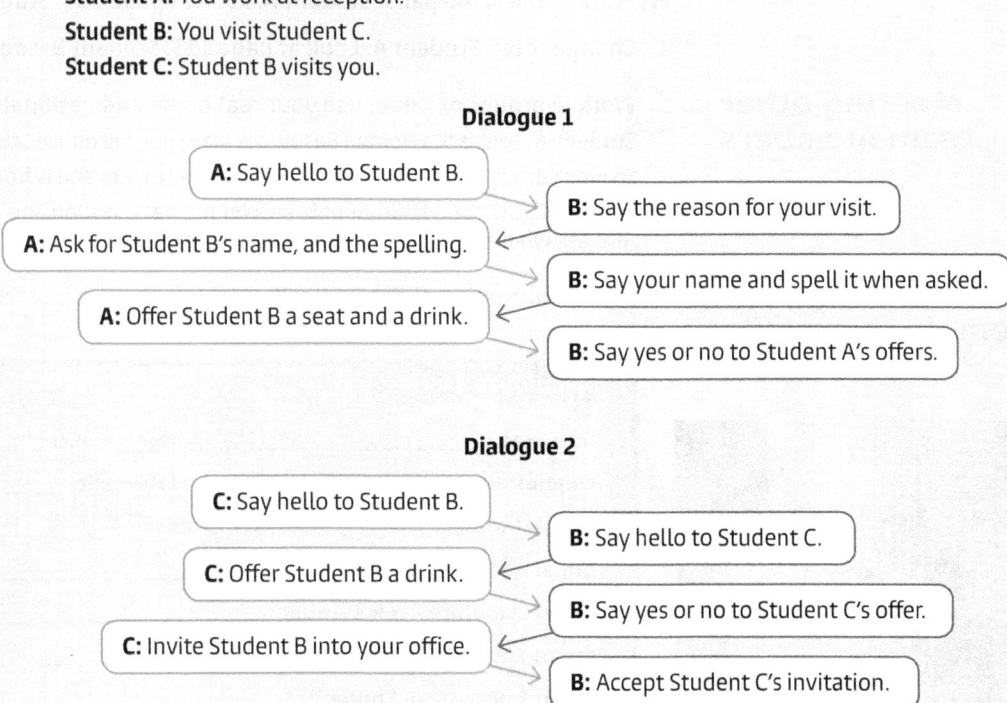

6 Practise the dialogues from Exercise 5.

Self-assessment I can introduce myself when visiting a company, greet visitors to my place of work and make simple offers.

BUSINESS WORKSHOP

Your first day

Lesson outcome Learners can introduce themselves in a new job for the first time, meet new colleagues and complete an employee profile.

Arriving

1 Work in pairs. It's your first day in a new job. Take turns being Student A and Student B.

Student A: You're the <u>receptionist</u>.
- Say hello to Student B.
- Ask for Student B's name, and the spelling.
- Offer Student B a seat and a drink.

Student B: You're the <u>new employee</u>.
- Say the reason for your visit.
- Say your name and spell it when asked.
- Say yes or no to Student A's offers.

Meeting human resources

2A Work in new pairs. Take turns being Student A and Student B. Follow the conversation outline below.

Student A: You are the <u>Human Resources Manager</u>. You know Student B.
Student B: You're the <u>new employee</u>. You know Student A.

Student A – Human Resources Manager

- Say hello. Say sorry to keep Student B waiting.
- Ask how Student B is.
- Answer, and then offer Student B a coffee.
- Invite Student B into your office.

Student B – new employee

- Say it's no problem and it's good to see Student A.
- Answer, then ask how Student A is.
- Say yes or no to Student A's offer.
- Say thank you.

B Work in the same pairs. Student A: Look at page 113. Student B: Look at page 115.

C Change roles. Student A: Look at page 115. Student B: Look at page 113.

Meeting other team members

3 Work in groups of three. Use your real name and nationality.

Student A: You're the Human Resources Manager. Introduce Student B and Student C.
Student B: Say hello to Student C and ask where he or she is from.
Student C: Say hello to Student B, answer his/her question and ask where he or she is from. Also ask where Student A is from.

Completing your employee profile

4 Write information about yourself.

Employee profile

Surname [1] _____ First name [2] _____
Gender: [3] male ◯ female ◯ other ◯ Nationality [4] _____
Marital status: [5] single ◯ married ◯ other ◯
Email address [6] _____
Phone / mobile / cell number [7] _____
Emergency contact number [8] _____
ID card or passport number [9] _____
Start date

Self-assessment I can introduce myself in a new job for the first time, meet new colleagues and complete an employee profile.

Work

Unit overview

2.1 What do you do?
Lesson outcome: Learners can understand and give a short basic description of common jobs.

Vocabulary: The work we do
Communicative grammar: Talking about work
Video: I work in Sales
Task: Where I work and what I do

2.2 What does the company do?
Lesson outcome: Learners can understand and give a short basic description of a company.

Vocabulary: What companies do
Reading and listening: Company information
Writing: Describing a company

2.3 A week in the life
Lesson outcome: Learners can write simple sentences about work routines and activities.

Reading: Two different routines
Communicative grammar: Talking about routines
Writing: A short blog post for a company intranet

2.4 Work skills: Small talk
Lesson outcome: Learners can talk about their jobs and work routines in a simple way.

Video: Small talk at work
Speaking: Making conversation

2.5 Business workshop: At a conference
Lesson outcome: Learners can introduce themselves in formal situations and talk about their companies and jobs in a simple way.

Reading: A conference website
Listening: Small talk at a conference
Speaking: Networking

Review 2: p.88 | Pronunciation: 2.2 Numbers 2.3 Questions p.97 | Grammar reference: 2.1 Talking about work 2.2 *a/an* 2.3 Talking about routines 2.4 Using *'s* and *s'* p.106

2.1 What do you do?

Lesson outcome — Learners can understand and give a short basic description of common jobs.

Lead-in

1 Look at the photos. Match the people (A–D) with the jobs.

| Digital Designer | IT Specialist | Production Engineer | Sales Manager |

A

B

C

D

Vocabulary — **The work we do**

2A Read the information about people and their jobs below. Match the person, job and department.

Name	Job	Department
Carla Lombardi	Production Engineer	sales
Ben Schmidt	Sales Manager	IT (information technology)
Lucas Sousa	IT Specialist	production
Anna Robinson	Digital Designer	marketing

B Complete the sentences with the correct name: Carla, Ben, Lucas or Anna.

1 _____ is German.
2 _____ works on projects.
3 _____ makes website designs.
4 _____ has meetings with clients.
5 _____ answers phone calls.
6 _____ sells transport services.
7 _____ solves technical problems.
8 _____ works in Milan.

 Teacher's resources: extra activities

Carla Lombardi

Where are you from?
I'm from Florence in Italy.

Where do you work?
I **work** for an e-commerce company. We **sell** sports clothes and equipment. I **work** in the Milan office.

What's your job?
I'm a Digital Designer. I **work** in the marketing department.

What do you do at work?
I **make** designs for the website and social media.

Ben Schmidt

Where are you from?
I'm from Hamburg in Germany.

Where do you work?
I **work** for a pharmaceutical company in Berlin. It's the capital of Germany.

What's your job?
I'm a Production Engineer.

What do you do at work?
I **check** the production processes are safe and cost-effective.

Lucas Sousa

Where are you from?
I'm from Brasília. It's the capital of Brazil.

Where do you work?
I **work** for Telefónica. It's a big telecommunications company.

What's your job?
I'm an IT Specialist and I **work** in the IT department.

What do you do at work?
I **work** on projects for other departments. I **solve** technical problems.

Anna Robinson

Where are you from?
I'm from Manchester in England.

Where do you work?
I **work** for a transport company.

What's your job?
I **work** as a Sales Manager.

What do you do at work?
I **manage** my sales team. I **have** twelve people in the team. I **make** and **answer** phone calls, **have** meetings with clients and **write** reports.

2.1 What do you do?

Communicative grammar

> **TALKING ABOUT WORK** → Grammar reference: page 106

I **work** in the marketing department.	She **works** in the marketing department.
You **manage** shop assistants.	He **writes** reports.
We **work** in a shop.	She **makes** designs.
They **sell** clothes.	He **sells** clothes.
I/You/We/They **have** meetings.	He/She **has** meetings.

3 Match 1–4 with a–d and 5–8 with e–h.

1 I manage   a phone calls to clients.
2 You work for   b hybrid and electric cars.
3 We sell   c a team of twelve people.
4 They make   d a multinational company.

5 I have   e technical problems.
6 You solve   f the process is safe.
7 We write   g meetings with clients.
8 They check   h emails and reports.

4 Complete the texts with the correct form of the verbs in the boxes.

| have   sell   work   write |

David is an Accountant. He ¹_____ for a chemical company. It ²_____ chemical products. He ³_____ meetings with other departments and he ⁴_____ financial reports.

| answer   manage   work   solve |

Linda ⁵_____ as a Customer Service Manager. She ⁶_____ a team of twenty staff. She ⁷_____ phone calls from customers and ⁸_____ their problems.

T Teacher's resources: extra activities

VIDEO **5A** ▶ 2.1.1 Watch Elena in the video and complete the information in the table.

	Elena	Ellen	Steve
City/Country	Southend-on-Sea	Leicester, England	⁹_____
Company	¹_____	⁵_____	¹⁰_____
Job/Department	²_____	Senior Research Manager	¹¹_____
Responsibilities	³_____ the phone, ⁴_____ and give visitors a pass	⁶_____ with the team and ⁷_____ with manager, make phone calls and ⁸_____ emails	¹²_____ the sales team, ¹³_____ meetings with clients

B Watch Ellen and complete the information in the table.

C Watch Steve and complete the information in the table.

TASK

6A Work in pairs. Ask and answer the questions.
- What's your name? • Where are you from? • Where do you work?
- What's your job? • What do you do at work?

Student A: Read your role card on page 114 or use your own information.
Student B: Read your role card on page 116 or use your own information.

B Work in new pairs. Use the questions in Exercise 6A and introduce yourself to your partner.

C Work with your partner from Exercise 6A. Tell your partner about the person you talked to in Exercise 6B.

His/Her name is …

Self-assessment I can understand and give a short basic description of common jobs.

2.2 What does the company do?

Lesson outcome — Learners can understand and give a short basic description of a company.

Lead-in

1 Do you have these products? What brand is the product?

| car   e-reader   laptop/computer   mobile phone   TV   washing machine |

Vocabulary What companies do

2A Match the photos (A–F) with the business activities.

| design cars   make clothes   make consumer electronics |
| provide air transport services   provide financial services   sell products online |

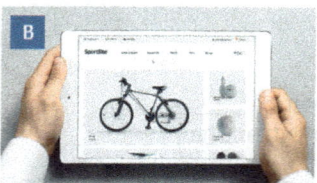

B Match the companies with the business activities in Exercise 2A.

| Allianz   Amazon   Inditex   Qatar Airways   Samsung   Volkswagen |

3 🔊 2.01 Choose the correct word. Then listen and check.
1 Qatar Airways *designs / provides* air transport services.
2 Allianz *provides / makes* financial services.
3 Volkswagen *designs / provides*, makes and sells cars.
4 Amazon *makes / sells* books and other products online.
5 Inditex makes and *sells / provides* clothes in shops and online.
6 Samsung *makes / provides* mobile phones and home electronics.

4A Write sentences about these companies using the verbs in Exercise 3.

| Alibaba   Apple   Bank of China   H&M   Lufthansa   Toyota |

B Work in pairs. Ask and answer questions about the companies.
A: What does Apple do?   **B:** It makes …

5A 🔊 2.02 Write the missing numbers. Then listen and repeat.

100	a/one hundred
_____	three hundred and twenty
647	six hundred _____ forty seven
1,000	a/one thousand
55,367	fifty-five _____, three _____ and sixty-seven
_____	seventy-eight thousand, one hundred and thirteen
100,000	a/one hundred thousand
360,000	three hundred _____ sixty _____
_____	eight hundred and ninety-two thousand, six hundred and seventeen
1,000,000	a/one million

➜ **page 112** See Numbers

| 150   220   7,000   174,000 |
| 100,000   140,000 |

B 🔊 2.03 Complete the sentences with the numbers in the box. Then listen and check.
Allianz has over [1] _____ employees in more than seventy countries.
Amazon has over [2] _____ warehouse robots.
Qatar Airways has [3] _____ aircraft and flies to over [4] _____ destinations.
Inditex has over [5] _____ stores and over [6] _____ employees in ninety-six countries.

C How many employees/students are there where you work/study?

Teacher's resources: extra activities

➜ **page 97** See Pronunciation bank: Numbers

2.2 What does the company do?

Reading and listening

Company information

6 Look at the company profile. Complete the table.

Company name	
Business	
Head office	
Number of countries	
Number of staff	
Top sales	

About Tramuntana

We are an e-commerce company. We sell clothes and shoes in our online shop. We work with top brands. We are based in Paris and have offices in eighteen countries. We have 700 staff all over the world. Most of our sales are in Brazil, Mexico, Spain, Poland, Germany and Ireland.

7 Read the company profile again. Are the sentences *true* (T) or *false* (F)? Correct the false sentences.

1 Tramuntana designs cars.
2 It sells products on the internet.
3 It sells famous brands.
4 It is an international company.
5 There are 700 staff in Paris.
6 The top sales are in Asia.

8 2.04 Listen to Alan Murray talking about his company. Match 1–5 with a–e.

1 We are
2 We provide
3 Our global head office is based
4 We have over 360 offices
5 We have

a in Bonn, Germany.
b an international transport company.
c in 220 countries.
d 85,000 staff and 250 aircraft.
e global logistics services.

> **A/AN** → Grammar reference: page 106
>
> We use *an* with a word beginning with a vowel sound: *an airline, an e-commerce company, an international transport company, an MBA, an hour, an online company*, etc.
>
> We use *a* with other words: *a bank, a car company, a manufacturer*, etc.

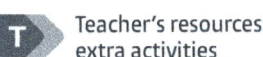 Teacher's resources: extra activities

Writing

9A Look at the table about the InterContinental Hotels Group. Write a short description of the company. Use some of the phrases in the box.

Company name	InterContinental Hotels Group (IHG)
Business	hospitality services
Head office	Denham, England
Hotels	Over 5,300
Countries	100
Staff	Over 375,000 people in hotels and corporate offices globally

> We are a/an … company.   We make/sell …   We provide … services.
> We are based in …   We have (offices) in …   We have over … staff/offices/etc.

B Work in pairs. Write a similar description about a different company. Use some of the phrases in the box.
Student A: turn to page 114.
Student B: turn to page 115.

C Compare your descriptions from Exercise 9B with your partner.

Self-assessment — I can understand and give a short basic description of a company.

2.3 A week in the life

Lesson outcome Learners can write simple sentences about work routines and activities.

Lead-in 1A Put the days of the week in order (1–7). Which days are the weekend?

Friday Monday *1* Saturday Sunday Thursday Tuesday Wednesday

B 🔊 2.05 Listen and check. Then listen again and repeat.

Reading 2 Complete the texts with questions a–i.

a Where are you from?
b Where **do** you **work**?
c What **do** you **do**? (x2)
d What **do** you **do** at work? (x2)
e **Do** you **like** your job? (x2)
f **Do** you **travel** for work?
g **Does** the company **have** offices in other countries?
h What days **do** you **work**?
i What **do** you **do** in your free time?

About Charlotte Thomas

1 _____
I'm an IT specialist.

2 _____
I work for a German company. It's a financial services provider. I'm based in the Guildford office in England.

3 _____
I work on projects for different departments. I design software programs and provide technical solutions.

4 _____
Yes, the projects are interesting.

5 _____
Yes, but I **don't travel** a lot. I go to the company head office in Munich every three months to see my boss. I spend a week there.

6 _____
Yes. Germany, the UK, the Netherlands and Japan.

THE WORK AND HOLIDAY BLOG
Meet Álvaro and Pablo

7 _____
We're students from Spain. We have visas to live, work and study in Australia for a year.

8 _____
We work in a restaurant in Sydney. We're waiters.

9 _____
We take food orders, prepare drinks and serve customers.

10 _____
Five days a week from Wednesday to Sunday. We **don't work** on Monday and Tuesday.

11 _____
We **don't work** in the morning, we study English. On Monday and Tuesday afternoon we go to the beach and relax.

12 _____
Yes, it's good work experience and we have money to study and travel.

3 Read the two texts again. Who does this information refer to?

	Charlotte	Álvaro and Pablo	All
1 travels/travel for work	✔		
2 likes/like the job			
3 works/work at the weekend			
4 works/work in an office			
5 studies/study			

2.3 A week in the life

Communicative grammar

TALKING ABOUT ROUTINES → Grammar reference: page 106

+ I/You/We/They **work** for a German company.
  I/You/We/They **live** in Australia.
  He/She **designs** software programs.
  He/She **spends** a week in Munich every three months.

− I/You/We/They **do not travel** for work.
  I/You/We/They **don't work** on Monday and Tuesday.
  He/She **does not work** in the head office.
  He/She **doesn't study** in the afternoon.

? **Do** you **travel** for work?
  Do they **like** their jobs?
  Does he/she **work** at the weekend?

? Where **do** you **work**?
  What **do** they **do** at work?
  What days **does** he/she **work**?

→ page 97 See Pronunciation bank: Questions

4A Choose the correct word.
1 He *don't / doesn't* work in an office.
2 I *don't / doesn't* live in Munich.
3 We *don't / doesn't* have visas.
4 He *don't / doesn't* travel for work.
5 You *don't / doesn't* work on Monday.
6 She *don't / doesn't* spend a month in Germany.
7 They *don't / doesn't* go to the beach at the weekend.
8 The IT department *don't / doesn't* have an office in London.

B Put the words in the correct order to make sentences.
1 not / websites / He / does / design
2 like / job / She / not / her / does
3 pizzas / have / The / does / not / restaurant
4 does / language / The / provide / college / not / classes
5 for / does / He / not / work / travel
6 does / food / She / not / the / prepare

5A Complete the questions with *do* or *does*.
1 What _____ Álvaro and Pablo study?
2 _____ Charlotte Thomas work in London?
3 Where _____ Álvaro and Pablo work?
4 How often _____ Charlotte go to Munich?
5 What days _____ Álvaro and Pablo work?
6 What _____ Charlotte do at work?

B Work in pairs. Ask and answer the questions in Exercise 5A.

6A Write questions with *you*.

1	What / do?	
2	Where / live?	
3	What / do at work?	
4	What days / work?	
5	work at the weekend?	
6	travel for work?	
7	like your job?	

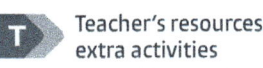
Teacher's resources: extra activities

B Work in pairs. Ask and answer the questions in Exercise 6A.

Writing

7 Write a short blog post for your company intranet. Choose one option.
1 Write about a new colleague at work.
2 You have a new job. Write about yourself.

Self-assessment I can write simple sentences about work routines and activities.

2.4 WORK SKILLS
Small talk

Lesson outcome — Learners can talk about their jobs and work routines in a simple way.

Lead-in 1A Match the photos with the situations.

> friends in a café   new colleagues by the coffee machine at work   strangers in a lift

B Look at the situations again. What do people talk about in each situation?

> family   free-time activities   health   home town
> job   nationality   nothing   the weather   work

C Think of some more things to talk about for each situation.

2 Use the phrases to complete the dialogue for photo A in Exercise 1A.

T: I'm Tony. ¹_____ (What / your name)?
S: Hi, I'm Susan. Nice to meet you.
T: ²_____ (Which department / you work in, Susan)?
S: Sales. I'm in Mark's team.
T: ³_____ (What / you do)?
S: ⁴_____ (I / a Sales Rep).
What about you? ⁵_____ (Where / you work)?
T: I work in the IT department.

VIDEO 3A ▶ 2.4.1 Watch the video without sound. Do the people in the video know each other well?

B Watch the video with sound. What do Andrea and Jack talk about?

4A Watch the video again and complete the table.

	Jack	Andrea
Department	¹_____	⁵_____
Job	Community ²_____	⁶_____ Director
Tasks	³_____ blogs provide images and videos for the website and for social media ⁴_____ messages from customers and write answers	⁷_____ meetings with sales team and big clients ⁸_____ to sales conferences in Europe every year

B Which job do you prefer, Andrea's or Jack's? Why?

24

2.4 Work skills: Small talk

> **USING 'S AND S'** → Grammar reference: page 107
>
> Mark**'s** team = Mark has a team, the company**'s** image = the company has an image
> The employee**s'** canteen = the employees have a canteen
> The customer**s'** email addresses = the customers have email addresses

5A Complete the sentences with one word in each gap. Watch the video again if necessary.
1 You're _____ here, right?
2 Yes, that's _____ . It's my first week.
3 Nice to _____ you.
4 Which _____ are you in?
5 What _____ a Community Manager do?
6 I write blogs and _____ images and videos.
7 That sounds _____ .
8 _____ do you work?
9 _____ you travel for work?
10 _____ talking to you.

B Work in pairs. Practise saying the sentences in Exercise 5A.

Speaking

> **MAKING SMALL TALK**
>
> **Starting a conversation**
> Hi! My name's …
> Hello, I'm …
> Nice to meet you (again).
>
> **Asking questions**
> Which department are you in?
> What do you do?
> Do you work (in finance / with Sylvia, etc.)?
> Do you know (Jack/Susan, etc.)?
>
> **Showing interest**
> Really?
> Oh, I see.
> That sounds interesting/boring/good/great, etc.
> That's interesting/boring/good/great, etc.
> What about you? / And you?
>
> **Finishing a conversation**
> Nice talking to you.
> See you later.
> See you soon.

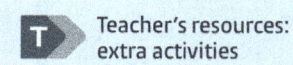

6A Work in pairs. Choose a role or complete the table for yourself. Write a dialogue between these people by the coffee machine at work. Use the Speaking box to help you.

Student A: You are Andrea, Jack or yourself.
Student B: You are a new person in the company. Choose a role: Oscar, Veronica or yourself.

	Oscar	Veronica	Me
Job	Intern	Admin Assistant	
Department	human resources	purchasing	
Tasks	answer phones, make photocopies, take notes at meetings, learn from colleagues	phone suppliers, make orders, write emails, solve problems with orders, check documents	

B Practise the dialogue.

Self-assessment: I can talk about my job and work routines in a simple way.

BUSINESS WORKSHOP

At a conference

Lesson outcome — Learners can introduce themselves in formal situations and talk about their companies and jobs in a simple way.

A conference website

1 Look at the website. Answer the questions.
1 Where is it? 2 When is it?

Global marketing conference
Where top professionals from all industries meet every year
London, 7–8 March

CONFERENCE PROGRAMME
CONFERENCE SPEAKERS
REGISTRATION

Conference small talk

2A Do you go to conferences? Do you have a business card?

B 🔊 2.06 Listen to a conversation at the Global marketing conference. Complete the business cards with the person's job. Do the people know each other?

Here's my card.

GND Group
Potsdamer Platz 5,
10785 Berlin, Germany

Anthony Kowalski
_____
Anthony.Kowalski@gndg.com
+49 30 200679740

abc Design Solutions
150 City Rd, London
EC1T 2NZ, UK

Patricia Williams
_____
📞 +44 20 7946 0316
✉ p.williams@abcd.com

3 Listen to the conversation again. What do they talk about? Tick (✓) five options from the box.

> their companies   their families   their home towns
> the hotel   their jobs   their nationalities   the weather

4A 🔊 2.07 Listen and complete the questions from the conversation. Use one word in each gap.

1 _____ are you from, Anthony?
2 What _____ you? You're American, right?
3 What do you _____ , Anthony?
4 What do you do at _____ ?
5 What _____ your company do?
6 Sorry, what's your name _____ ?
7 Patricia, _____ do you do?
8 What _____ a Digital Project Manager do?
9 Do you _____ for work?

B Listen again and repeat the questions in Exercise 4A.

Networking

5 Look at page 122 and follow the instructions.

Self-assessment — I can introduce myself in formal situations and talk about my company and job in a simple way.

What? When? Where?

Unit overview

3.1	**We're very busy in December** **Lesson outcome:** Learners can talk about their routines and the busy periods in their jobs.	**Vocabulary:** Months and seasons **Communicative grammar:** Talking about ability and possibility **Video:** I can work flexible hours **Task:** Asking and talking about your partner's work
3.2	**Requests** **Lesson outcome:** Learners can make and reply to requests.	**Vocabulary:** Ordinal numbers and dates **Reading and listening:** Can I have some time off? **Speaking:** Talking about taking time off
3.3	**I am writing to complain …** **Lesson outcome:** Learners can write a short email describing a problem and requesting action.	**Reading:** Complaints **Communicative grammar:** Talking about the past **Writing:** An email to describe a problem and request action
3.4	**Work skills:** We have a problem **Lesson outcome:** Learners can describe problems in a simple way and explain solutions.	**Video:** A progress meeting **Speaking:** A progress meeting
3.5	**Business workshop:** A problem with a client **Lesson outcome:** Learners can identify problems, explain solutions and make and reply to requests.	**Reading:** A customer complaint **Speaking:** A problem-solving meeting; A phone call

Review 3: p.89 | **Pronunciation:** 3.1 *can* and *can't* 3.2 ordinal numbers p.98 | **Grammar reference:** 3.1 Talking about ability and possibility; *at, in, on, from … to …* 3.2 *Can … ?/Could … ?* 3.3 Talking about the past p.107

3.1 We're very busy in December

Lesson outcome — Learners can talk about their routines and the busy periods in their jobs.

Lead-in

1 Match the photos with the seasons.

autumn   spring
summer   winter

A · B · C · D

Vocabulary   Months and seasons

April   August   December
February   January   June
July   March   May
November   October
September

2A 🔊 3.01 Put the months in order. Then listen and check.

B Match the seasons in Exercise 1 with the months in Exercise 2A.

C What months are busy in your job?

3A 🔊 3.02 Listen to Emily and Mark talking about their jobs. Write the correct name next to each picture.

A _____   B _____

B Listen again. Are the sentences *true* (T) or *false* (F)?

Emily
1 We're never busy in March or April.
2 Winter is always quiet so I usually go on holiday in July or August.
3 I always go on holiday in spring.
4 I **can** speak Japanese.

Mark
5 November and December are busy.
6 I usually go on holiday in March, April or May.
7 I **can** go on holiday in summer.
8 I **can't** speak Spanish.

Communicative grammar

> **TALKING ABOUT ABILITY AND POSSIBILITY**   → Grammar reference: page 107
>
> \+ I/You/He/She/It/We/They **can** speak seven languages.
>   I/You/He/She/It/We/They **can** go on holiday in spring.
>
> − I/You/He/She/It/We/They **can't** speak other languages.
>   I/You/He/She/It/We/They **can't** finish work at 2 p.m.
>
> ? **Can** I/you/he/she/it/we/they speak Japanese?
>   Yes, I/you/he/she/it/we/they **can**. / No, I/you/he/she/it/we/they **can't**.
>   **Can** I/you/he/she/it/we/they go on holiday in January?
>   Yes, I/you/he/she/it/we/they **can**. / No, I/you/he/she/it/we/they **can't**.

→ page 98 See Pronunciation bank: *can* and *can't*

3.1 We're very busy in December

4 🔊 3.03 Complete the office rules with *can* and *can't*. Then listen and check.

In the new flexi-time system, staff need to work thirty-seven hours a week. They ¹_____ choose when they start and finish work and they ²_____ decide when to go to lunch.

- All employees need to be in the office from 10.30 a.m. to 3 p.m.
- This means employees ³_____ start after 10.30 a.m.
- They ⁴_____ finish work before 3 p.m.
- The building opens at 7 a.m. so employees ⁵_____ start work then.
- Employees ⁶_____ take one hour for lunch from 11.15 a.m. to 2.45 p.m.
- They ⁷_____ take lunch before 11.15 a.m. or after 2.45 p.m.
- They ⁸_____ work until 8 p.m. when the building closes.
- Remember, if you drive to work, you ⁹_____ only park your car in spaces 120–225.
- Employees need their ID card or they ¹⁰_____ enter the car park.

5 🔊 3.04 There are different ways to tell the time. Listen and tick (✓) the one you hear.

	1 **10:00**	2 **22:00**	3 **12.00**	4 **19.30**
	ten a.m. ☐ ten o'clock ☐	ten p.m. ☐ ten o'clock ☐	twelve ☐ twelve o'clock ☐	seven thirty ☐ half past seven ☐
	5 **03.15**	6 **11:45**	7 **20.10**	8 **16.40**
	three fifteen ☐ quarter past three ☐	eleven forty-five ☐ quarter to twelve ☐	eight ten ☐ ten past eight ☐	four forty ☐ twenty to five ☐

We can use the twenty-four-hour clock to talk about schedules, e.g. at the airport.
The flight is at 20.45 (= twenty forty-five).

> **AT, IN, ON, FROM … TO …** → Grammar reference: page 107
>
> **at** + time
> **at** 3.30, **at** 11 o'clock
>
> **in** + month, season, year, part of the day
> **in** June, **in** autumn, **in** 2020, **in** the morning
>
> **on** + day, date, special day, official holidays
> **on** Friday, **on** the 19th of June 2020, **on** my birthday, **on** New Year's Day
>
> **from** + day, time, date **to** + day, time, date
> **from** Monday **to** Friday, **from** 10 o'clock **to** 6 o'clock, **from** the 15th **to** the 31st of August

T Teacher's resources: extra activities

VIDEO

6A ▶ 3.1.1 Watch Part 1 of the video. Are the sentences *true* (T) or *false* (F)?

1. Fi usually works from 2.30 to 5.30.
2. Fi can't work flexible hours.
3. Fi can speak three languages.
4. Fi never goes on holiday in December.
5. Ellie usually finishes work at 5.30 p.m.
6. Ellie has a meeting with her manager on Mondays at 12.00.
7. Ellie can't go on holiday in September.

B Watch Part 2 of the video. Answer the questions.

1. What time does Kathryn start work?
2. When does Kathryn have team meetings?
3. When is her busy period?
4. When can she go on holiday?

> TASK

7A Work in pairs. Use the ideas in the box to ask questions about your partner's work.

| what time / start/finish work?   when / busy?   busy / spring?   when / go for lunch?   when / go on holiday? |

A: When can you go on holiday? **B:** We can go on holiday in spring, so I usually go on holiday in April.

B Now explain your partner's work to a new partner.
A: Susana can go on holiday in spring, so she usually goes on holiday in April.

Self-assessment | I can talk about my routine and the busy periods in my job. 🙂 🙁

29

3.2 Requests

Lesson outcome — Learners can make and reply to requests.

Lead-in 1 What's your favourite company? Why?

Vocabulary Ordinal numbers and dates

2A 🔊 3.05 Listen and complete the list with the company names in the box.

| Apple | Berkshire Hathaway | ExxonMobil | General Electric |
| Microsoft | Novartis | PetroChina | ~~Toyota Motor Corporation~~ |

FT Global 500 – World's top companies in 2015

	Company	Country	Value ($bn)
1st	_____	USA	724.7
2nd	_____	USA	356.5
3rd	_____	USA	356.5
4th	Google	USA	345.8
5th	_____	USA	333.5
6th	_____	China	329.7
7th	Wells Fargo	USA	279.9
8th	Johnson & Johnson	USA	279.7
9th	Industrial and Commercial Bank of China	China	275.3
10th	_____	Switzerland	267.8
11th	China Mobile	Hong Kong	267.2
12th	Wal-Mart Stores	USA	265.1
13th	_____	USA	249.7
14th	Nestlé	Switzerland	243.7
15th	Toyota Motor Corporation	Japan	238.9
16th	Acme Digital	USA	221.6

B The list in Exercise 2A is from 2015. Which companies do you think are first, second and third today? What other companies do you think are on the list today?

Look, there are no big e-commerce companies on this list! I think Amazon or Alibaba are on the list today.

C Work in pairs. Practise saying the numbers from 1st to 15th. Then try to say the numbers in the box.

| 16th | 18th | 20th | 21st | 22nd | 23rd | 27th | 30th | 31st | 40th | 100th | 500th |

1st – first, 2nd – second, ... 20th – twentieth, ... 23rd – twenty-third

3 🔊 3.06 Listen and <u>underline</u> the number you hear.
1. Our department always has a meeting on the *1st / 3rd* Thursday of the month.
2. Mr Barker's office is on the *22nd / 32nd* floor.
3. The delivery arrives on the *10th / 12th* of November.
4. Can you come to Sam's *13th / 30th* birthday on Monday?
5. That's the *15th / 50th* email today.
6. My holiday starts on the *9th / 19th* of July.
7. Thank you for waiting, you are *5th / 15th* in line.
8. I'm out of the office from the *12th / 20th* of January for a week.

4A 🔊 3.07 Listen and write the dates you hear.
1. 14/9/2021
2. _____
3. _____
4. _____
5. _____
6. _____
7. _____

B Work in pairs. Practise saying the dates in Exercise 4A.

14/9/2021 – the fourteenth of September twenty twenty-one

Say years in two parts:
1814 'eighteen fourteen'
1945 'nineteen forty-five'
2019 'twenty nineteen'.
But 2000 is 'two thousand' and 2001–2009 are 'two thousand and one', etc.

3.2 | Requests

19	13	60
10	50	1

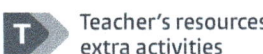
Teacher's resources: extra activities

5 🔊 3.08 Play bingo. Listen and circle the numbers as you hear them.
Student A: Look at the bingo card on the left.
Student B: Look at the bingo card on page 113.
Student C: Look at the bingo card on page 116.
Student D: Look at the bingo card on page 118.

➡ page 98 See Pronunciation bank: Ordinal numbers

Reading and listening

Can I have some time off?

6 Read the email. What does Michaela want? Why?

> Hi Colin,
> Good news! We move house on Tuesday 19th July.
> Could I please take some time off from Monday 18th to Thursday 21st July for the move? And could I also take Friday 15th July to prepare?
> Can you let me know as soon as possible? I need to start organising things!
> Thanks,
> Michaela

CAN … ?/COULD … ? ➡ Grammar reference: page 107

Requests
Use *could* to make polite requests.
Could I please take some time off?
Could you finish the report before you go?

Use *can* for requests in informal situations.
Can I take some time off?
Can you finish the report for me?

Replies
To reply positively, use: *Yes, of course (I/we can)*.
To reply negatively but politely, use:
I'm sorry but we **can't**.   **I'm afraid** you **can't**.   We **can't**. **I'm sorry**.   We **can't, I'm afraid**.

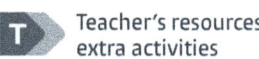
Teacher's resources: extra activities

7 🔊 3.09 Listen to Colin's phone call with Michaela. Answer the questions.
1 Does Colin give Michaela some time off?
2 How many people are on holiday in July?
3 What dates does Colin suggest for Michaela's holiday?
4 What does Colin ask Michaela to do?

8 Match 1–6 with a–f.
1 Could I please take
2 You can take from
3 I'm afraid you can't take
4 Could you let me know
5 Could I also take Friday
6 Can you finish

a as soon as possible?
b Monday 18th to Wednesday 20th.
c all the days you want.
d the report before you go?
e some time off?
f 15th July?

Speaking

9 Work in pairs.
Student A: Look at page 114 and read the information.
Student B: Look at page 119 and read the information.

Self-assessment   I can make and reply to requests. 🙂 🙁

3.3 I am writing to complain …

Lesson outcome — Learners can write a short email describing a problem and requesting action.

Lead-in 1 Match 1–5 with A–E.

What's wrong?

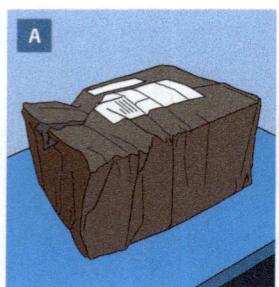 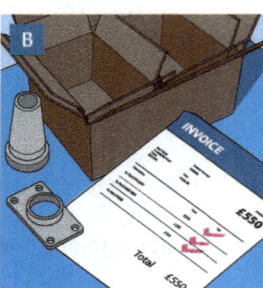   

1 My delivery is **late**. _C_
2 The product is **broken**. ____
3 The package is **damaged**. ____
4 An item is **missing**. ____
5 The price is **incorrect**. ____

Reading 2A What problems in Exercise 1 are complaints i–iv about? One problem is <u>not</u> used.

How can we help?

i	Our order **was** three parts, not two! Only two parts **were** in the box, the third **wasn't** there.	*An item is missing.*
ii	The price on the website **was** $250 but the price on the invoice **was** $300.	
iii	Our delivery **was** 8–11 a.m. I **was** here, but my packages **weren't**!	
iv	My new laptop **was** broken. The package and box **were** both OK, but the screen **was** damaged.	

B Use the questions 1–4 to continue the complaints in Exercise 2A.
1 _iii_ What time is the delivery? 3 ____ What is the correct price?
2 ____ Where is the missing part? 4 ____ When can you send me a new laptop?

Communicative grammar

> **TALKING ABOUT THE PAST** → Grammar reference: page 108

+ I/He/She **was** late for work.	− I/He/She **wasn't** (= **was not**) late for work.
You/We/They **were** late for work.	You/We/They **weren't** (= **were not**) late for work.
It **was** broken.	It **wasn't** broken.
There was a problem with the order.	**There was no** problem with the invoice.
There were three late deliveries in January.	**There were no** late deliveries in February.

? **Were** you/they at work yesterday?	+/− Yes, I/he/she **was**. / No, I/he/she **wasn't** (= **was not**).
Was he/she at work yesterday?	Yes, we/they **were**. / No, we/they **weren't** (= **were not**).
Was it broken?	Yes, it **was**. / No, it **wasn't** (= **was not**).
Was there a late delivery yesterday?	Yes, **there was**. / No, **there wasn't** (= **was not**).
Were there items missing?	Yes, **there were**. / No, **there weren't** (= **were not**).

Why **was** the invoice wrong?
Where **were** the missing items?

3.3 I am writing to complain ...

3 Choose the correct word.
1 There *was / were* a problem with the order.
2 How many items *was / were* missing?
3 The delivery *wasn't / weren't* correct.
4 My items *was / were* broken.
5 The delivery address on the invoice *was / were* wrong.
6 *Was / Were* there three computers in the package?
7 There *was / were* five items missing.
8 Two items *was / were* late, and one *was / were* broken.

4 Write questions with *was* and *were*.
1 What / the problem? _____
2 Why / the packages damaged? _____
3 When / the meeting? _____
4 Where / the reports? _____
5 he / in the meeting / yesterday? _____
6 Where / the order? _____

Teacher's resources: extra activities

5A Read the email. Which of the problems in Exercise 1 does Beata have?

From: Beata Minari
Beata.Minari@TPY.comm
Subject: Missing order

Dear Sir/Madam,
I am writing to complain about the order (Ref: 13267B) from Monday last week.
Our order ¹_____ three different parts. Unfortunately, only two parts ²_____ in yesterday's delivery – parts RJY4653 and PHG847 ³_____ both in the box, but NBG7896 ⁴_____ . Where is the missing part?
This third item is now one week late, and this is a big problem for us.
Can you ᵃ_____ , please?
I look forward to hearing from you.
Best regards,
Beata Minari
Purchase Manager, TPY Inc.

B Complete gaps 1–4 in the email with *was(n't)* or *were(n't)*.

C Read the requests below. Then look at gap a in the email. Which two requests can Beata use?

Can you [change the part, / send the missing item, / send a different item, / resend the invoice, / send the correct order,] please?

Writing

6 Put the phrases in the correct order. Use the email in Exercise 5A to help you.
a I look forward to hearing from you. ____
b Best regards, ____
c I am writing to complain about ... ____
d Dear ... , ____

7 Look at the situations ii–iv in Exercise 2A. Choose one and write an email like the one in Exercise 5A. Remember to:
• use the phrases from Exercise 6 in your email.
• describe the problem.
• request action.

Self-assessment I can write a short email describing a problem and requesting action.

3.4 WORK SKILLS
We have a problem

Lesson outcome Learners can describe problems in a simple way and explain solutions.

Lead-in

1 Look at the photos. Complete the types of meeting (a–c) with the words in the box.

planning   progress   problem-solving

a   a _____ meeting

The project starts next month.
Mike, what is the budget for testing?
This is a new project team, so let's start with introductions.

b   a _____ meeting

Does anyone have an idea?
Why not make a new product?
We could change the website design.
How can we fix this?

c   a _____ meeting

Where are we with the project?
We're a week late and we need to hire more people.
There's a problem with the schedule.

VIDEO

2A Match the problems 1–3 with the solutions a–c.
1 can't find parts at a good price
2 people are on holiday in summer
3 website doesn't work properly

a ask an IT specialist for help
b hire more people in July and August
c use big, international suppliers

B Match the problems/solutions in Exercise 2A with the items on the agenda (i–iii).

C ▶ 3.4.1 Watch the meeting. Who can meet their deadline? Who can't?

Team meeting:
10 June, 10.00–10.30, room 5

AGENDA
i   Project planning
ii New supplier
iii Online invoice system
Any other business

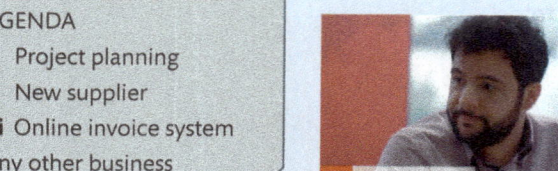
Paulo

Rachel

Martin

3.4 Work skills: We have a problem

3 Put the words in bold in the correct order. Watch the video again if necessary.

1 Paulo, **with are where we** planning the new project?

2 **aren't we finished**. I'm sorry.

3 And Rachel, **situation the what's with** finding a new supplier?

4 OK, **what we do can** to solve this?

5 **Can finish we** on schedule?

6 No. I think **time we more need**.

7 Martin, **you about tell can us** the online invoicing system?

8 We **a with problem have** the website, but **we solve can** it.

9 **we're schedule on**.

Speaking

> **A PROGRESS MEETING**

Talking about progress
Where are you/we with planning the new project?   We aren't / It isn't finished.
What's the situation with the product testing?   We're/It's on schedule.

Talking about problems
The problem is they can't make the parts we need.
We have a problem with the website.
There was a problem with the invoices.

Talking about solutions
What can we do to solve this?   We can look for international suppliers.
How can we fix this?   We need to change how the system works.
    We can see the solution.
    We can solve it.

Talking about schedules
Is everything on schedule?   Yes, I think we can finish it by Friday.
Can you/we finish by next week?   I think we need more time, I'm sorry.
Can you/we meet the deadline?

Teacher's resources: extra activities

Team meeting:

AGENDA
i Car design
ii Supplier
iii Website
Any other business

4 Work in groups of four. You all work in a car company. Look at the agenda and have a team progress meeting.
Student A: Look at page 119 and read the information.
Student B: Look at page 113 and read the information.
Student C: Look at page 115 and read the information.
Student D: Look at page 117 and read the information.

Self-assessment   I can describe problems in a simple way and explain solutions.

BUSINESS WORKSHOP

A problem with a client

Lesson outcome — Learners can identify problems, explain solutions and make and reply to requests.

A customer complaint

1 Read the email and choose the correct words.
1 The order yesterday was *correct / incorrect*.
2 *Three / Five* parts were not in the package yesterday.
3 The other parts in the order yesterday were *right / wrong*.
4 This is the *first / second* time the delivery was late.
5 GKB Production want *the missing parts / different parts*.

C.Charleston <Chris.Charls@GKB.co.uk>
Order 45231C

Dear Sir/Madam,

I am writing to complain about our order (Ref. 45231C) yesterday from Denilson's.

Unfortunately, the order was wrong. Three parts were missing and the other parts were incorrect. The package was also two hours late.

This is the first time there was a problem with late delivery, but it is the third time there was a problem with an order. Last month, all the parts in our order were broken and last week five of the items were missing.

This is a big problem for us. Can you send us the missing parts and improve delivery for the next order, please?

I look forward to hearing from you.

Best regards,

Chris Charleston,

Purchasing Manager, GKB Production

A problem-solving meeting

2 Read your role card and prepare for the meeting.

Student A: Follow the instructions on this page.
Student B: Look at page 113 and follow the instructions.

Student A
Work with another Student A. Put the bold words in the correct order.

1 **with are where we** GKB? _____
2 **we fix how can** this? _____
3 **with the what's situation** the delivery company? _____
4 **change can we** the delivery company? _____
5 **find you can** a solution this week? _____
6 **give we can** GKB a discount on their next three orders. _____

Read your role card and prepare for the meeting with your employee.

> You are the Sales Manager at Denilson's.
> • Meet your employee. He/She is a Sales Rep and GKB Production is his/her client.
> • Discuss the delivery problems with him/her.
> • Use the agenda and try to include the sentences above in your conversation.
> • Agree on possible solutions and a time to visit GKB together.

Work in Student A/B pairs. Have the meeting.

> **AGENDA**
> 1 Discuss the problems with the GKB delivery.
> 2 Discuss possible solutions.

A phone call

3 Work with a partner.

Student A: Follow the instructions on this page.
Student B: Look at page 115 and follow the instructions.

Student A
You are the Sales Manager at Denilson's. Your employee, the Sales Representative for Denilson's, calls you to ask for something. Listen to his/her request and use the information below in your call.

• The Sales Representative doesn't need to go to the meeting at GKB.
• You have a meeting with the CEO on Monday 12th May at 2 p.m.
• You are on holiday on Friday 9th May, so you need to know about the new delivery company on Thursday 8th May.

Self-assessment — I can identify problems, explain solutions and make and reply to requests.

Problems and solutions

4

Unit overview

4.1	**What went wrong?** **Lesson outcome:** Learners can talk about problems at work in the past.	**Vocabulary:** Past irregular verbs **Communicative grammar:** Talking about the past **Video:** Problems at work **Task:** Talking about problems in the past and how you solved them
4.2	**How can I help?** **Lesson outcome:** Learners can make simple phone calls describing problems and offering solutions.	**Vocabulary:** Solutions **Listening:** On the phone **Speaking and writing:** Making phone calls at work
4.3	**We are sorry that …** **Lesson outcome:** Learners can reply in a simple way to an email of complaint.	**Reading:** An email of complaint and a reply **Communicative grammar:** Using negatives in the past; Asking questions about the past **Writing:** A reply email
4.4	**Work skills:** Face-to-face complaints **Lesson outcome:** Learners can say sorry in work-related contexts.	**Video:** There is a problem with … **Speaking:** Responding to a complaint
4.5	**Business workshop:** Can I help you? **Lesson outcome:** Learners can make and receive simple phone calls about problems at work and understand and reply to emails of complaint.	**Speaking:** Making phone calls **Reading:** An email of complaint **Writing:** Replying to a complaint

Review 4: p.90 | **Pronunciation:** 4.1 The *-ed* ending 4.3 'th' as /θ/ and /ð/ p.99 | **Grammar reference:** 4.1 Talking about the past: Past Simple 4.2 Making offers and promises with *will* 4.3 Using negatives and questions in the past: Past Simple p.108

4.1 What went wrong?

Lesson outcome   Learners can talk about problems at work in the past.

Lead-in

1 Read the problems people have at work. Which sentences are true for you?
1 I sometimes write the wrong address on an email.
2 I often send emails to the wrong person.
3 People sometimes give me the wrong contact information.
4 We always have problems with the internet.
5 I never say that person's name correctly. Is it Grzmiel?
6 I sometimes make mistakes on an invoice.
7 I often see spelling mistakes in emails.
8 I'm always late for meetings.

Vocabulary Past irregular verbs

2A ▶ 4.01 Look at the pictures. Complete 1–5 with a–e. Then listen and check.

a I **made** a mistake on an invoice.
b I **sent** the report after the deadline.
c I **went** to the wrong office this morning.
d The headphones stopped working.
e Tom was late, but he **said** sorry when he arrived.

1 ____ I **saw** the people talking but there was no sound.
2 ____ The project was delayed. 
3 ____ We **had** a meeting at 3 p.m. yesterday. ____ 
4 ____ I **wrote** the wrong address last week. ____ 
5 ____ The client complained and we **gave** him the money back. 

B Complete the second sentence in each pair with the pink verbs in Exercise 2A.
1 I go to work at 7 a.m. every day. I ____went____ to work at 8 a.m. yesterday.
2 I usually make two or three phone calls a day. Yesterday, I _____ ten phone calls.
3 I often write emails to my clients. I _____ thirty emails to clients last week.
4 He says a lot in meetings. He _____ a lot in the meeting yesterday.
5 She sends invoices every day. She _____ twenty invoices yesterday.
6 We have a meeting every day. We _____ two meetings yesterday.
7 You see your manager every day. You _____ your manager last week.
8 We give new clients a discount. I _____ two clients a discount yesterday.

T Teacher's resources: extra activities

Communicative grammar

> **TALKING ABOUT THE PAST**   → Grammar reference: page 108
>
> **Past regular verbs**
> I/You/He/She/We/They **work**ed late last night.
> I/You/He/She/We/They **stop**ped working on Mondays last week.
> I/You/He/She/We/They **stud**ied finance at university.
> It **start**ed last year.
>
> **Past irregular verbs**
> be → was/were; give → gave; go → went; have → had; make → made; say → said; see → saw; send → sent; write → wrote

→ **page 104** See Irregular verbs list
→ **page 99** See Pronunciation bank: The -ed ending

4.1 What went wrong?

3 Complete the sentences with the past form of the words in brackets. The verbs are regular.
1 I _____ (work) in Paris last year.
2 I _____ (manage) a big team last month.
3 She _____ (miss) the meeting this morning.
4 They _____ (provide) our internet last year.
5 I _____ (travel) to work by car last week.
6 I _____ (stop) working in sales two months ago.
7 I _____ (study) finance at university.
8 We _____ (press) the button and the photocopier stopped working.

4A Complete the text with the past form of the words in brackets. Some verbs are irregular.

We ¹_____ (have) an important client presentation but we ²_____ (make) a mistake on the slides. The wrong client's name was on them! We ³_____ (change) the name and ⁴_____ (give) a copy of the new slides to everyone at the presentation but we ⁵_____ (send) the old presentation with the wrong name to the client by email.

B Complete the text with the past form of the words in the box. Some verbs are irregular.

| go   have   miss   not be   say   write |

I ¹_____ a meeting with a client at 100A Piccadilly in London, but I ²_____ 101A. I ³_____ to the meeting but there ⁴_____ a 101A! I ⁵_____ the meeting. I called the client and ⁶_____ sorry.

Teacher's resources: extra activities

VIDEO

5 ▶ 4.1.1 Watch the video of people talking about problems at work. Put the three sentences for each person in the correct order.

Leonora
a I called the IT specialist.   ____
b I checked the paper.   ____
c I turned it off and on.   ____

Rob
a I telephoned the client.   ____
b I arrived an hour late.   ____
c I went by metro.   ____

Ali
a I sent more and more emails.   ____
b The client sent the documents.   ____
c I called the client.   ____

6A Work in pairs. Tell your partner about Leonora's, Rob's or Ali's problem and how they solved it.

>TASK

B Work in pairs. Choose a problem from the box or use the notes for Student A and B. What was your partner's problem?
Student A: Look at page 114. Student B: Look at page 122.

| A train or plane was late.   You made a mistake on an invoice or a report.   You missed a deadline.   You went to the wrong building.   Your computer stopped working.   Other. |

C Tell your partner's story to a new partner.

Self-assessment I can talk about problems at work in the past.   ☺ ☹

39

4.2 How can I help?

Lesson outcome: Learners can make simple phone calls describing problems and offering solutions.

Lead-in

1 Work in pairs. How often do you have these problems?
1. An invoice has the wrong information.
2. You don't receive an important email.
3. An order is lost.
4. There's no ink for the printer.
5. A delivery is late.
6. You forget your phone charger.
7. The sound doesn't work in a video call.
8. You can't find a client's office.

never → once or twice a month → a few times a week → sometimes → every day → all the time

Vocabulary Solutions

2 Look at the solutions (a–h). Which problem in Exercise 1 does each one solve?

a **Ask** a colleague **for** a charger. _6_
b **Ask** a colleague **to** check the address. ____
c **Check** your spam folder. ____
d **Check that** your headphones work. ____
e **Contact** the delivery company **about** the order. ____
f **Contact** the supplier **by** email. ____
g **Send** the driver a message. ____
h **Send** an order **to** your supplier. ____

3A Choose the correct word.
1. **A:** I can't find the email from Bronson Ltd.
   B: Are you sure? Do you need to *check / contact* your spam folder?
2. **A:** We don't have any ink left.
   B: OK, I can contact our supplier *for / about* the order.
3. **A:** I need to finish this report.
   B: You can ask Chris *about / to* help you.
4. **A:** My order is three days late.
   B: Why don't you *send / contact* the delivery company?

ask ... to   check that
contact ... about

B Complete the text with the past form of the words in the box. The verbs are regular.

I had a video call but there was no sound on the computer. I ¹_____ the headphones worked but there was still no sound. I ²_____ a colleague _____ help me and the headphones worked on her computer. I ³_____ IT _____ the problem and they fixed it, but I missed the call.

C Write a solution for each problem.
1. I can't find the email from the supplier. (check / spam folder)
   Check your spam folder.
2. I lost my ID card. (ask / your manager / a new one)
   _____
3. My keyboard doesn't work. (check / it's connected to the computer)
   _____
4. John never answers his phone. (send / him / a message)
   _____
5. The order is wrong. (contact / the supplier / phone)
   _____
6. My computer doesn't work. (ask / IT / help you)
   _____
7. The invoice is wrong. (contact / the supplier / the invoice)
   _____
8. The printer doesn't work. (send / the document / a different printer)
   _____

Teacher's resources: extra activities

4.2 | How can I help?

Listening

On the phone

4 🔊 4.02 Listen to a phone call and complete Maria's notes.

> Sandra Dennison from
> ¹_____ phoned.
> Wrong information on
> the ²_____ .
> Can you call her on
> 45 ³_____ ?

5A Complete the words.
1. How can I h ___ you?
2. Could I s ____ to Chris, please?
3. I'm a _____ Chris is in a meeting.
4. Can I t ___ a message?
5. T ___ is Sandra Dennison from ATQ Global.
6. I'm sorry a ____ that.
7. Could you a __ Chris to call me?
8. Is that r ____?
9. I'll g ___ Chris the message.
10. C __ I help you with anything else?

B 🔊 4.03 Listen and check. Then listen again and repeat.

> **MAKING OFFERS AND PROMISES WITH WILL** → Grammar reference: page 108
>
> I/You/He/She/We/They**'ll call** (= I/You/He/She/We/They **will call**) you back.
> **I'll give** (= **I will give**) Chris the message.
> **I'll send** (= **I will send**) you a copy of the invoice.

6 🔊 4.04 Listen to Chris return Sandra's call. Tick (✓) the solution Chris offers.

| to add an item to the order | to create a new order | to give Sandra her money back |

7A Put the bold words in the correct order.
1. Hi, Chris. **Sandra is this**.   _This is Sandra._
2. Hi, Sandra. **call returning I'm your**.   _____
3. So **I'm have we afraid only** a record of the black ink.   _____
4. **add I can** the colour ink to your order now.   _____
5. **create I'll a invoice new**.   _____
6. **you send I'll copy a** of the new invoice today. _____
7. No. **can I the team ask** to add it to your order. _____
8. Can **help I you anything with** else?   _____

B 🔊 4.05 Listen and check. Then listen again and repeat.

Speaking and writing

8 Work in groups of three.
Student A: Look at page 114. Student B: Look at page 116. Student C: Look at page 118.

Teacher's resources: extra activities

Self-assessment: I can make simple phone calls describing problems and offering solutions.

4.3 We are sorry that ...

Lesson outcome: Learners can reply in a simple way to an email of complaint.

Lead-in 1 Tick (✓) the reasons you write emails. Then tell your partner.

| apologise to a customer | arrange a meeting | ask for / give information |
| complain | contact friends and family | request action | solve problems | other |

Reading 2 Read the email and answer the questions.
1 Why does Mr Taylor write the email?
2 What was the problem?
3 What does Mr Taylor want?

✉
From: M. Taylor
matthew.taylor@PAL.com
Subject: Broken printer

I am writing to complain about the printer/photocopier (Model: 13267B) we received last week.
Unfortunately, the machine worked for three days but then the paper ran out. After we put more paper in, the machine turned on, but it **didn't copy** documents and **didn't work** when we needed to print from our computers.
Can you replace the machine, please?
I look forward to hearing from you.
Best regards,
Matthew Taylor
Office Manager, PAL Pet Insurance

Communicative grammar

> **USING NEGATIVES IN THE PAST**   → Grammar reference: page 108
>
> I/You/He/She/We/They **didn't finish** (= I/You/He/She/We/They **did not finish**) the report.
> The printer **didn't print** (= **did not print**).
> The photocopier **didn't copy** (= **did not copy**).

3 Rewrite the sentences using the past negative form. Remember to check the irregular verbs on page 104.

1 The technician came. _The technician didn't come._
2 My computer worked. _____
3 You lost your headphones. _____
4 I had a problem. _____
5 The delivery arrived. _____
6 They complained. _____

Teacher's resources: extra activities

Reading 4A Read the reply to the email in Exercise 2. What does the company want to do next?

✉
From: F. Franchesa
Federico.Franchesa@Zafusi.com
Subject: Broken printer

Dear Mr Taylor,
We are sorry that your printer/photocopier doesn't work.
To help us solve your problem, can we get some more information?
• **Did** you **check** that there was ink in the printer/photocopier?
• **Did** you **try** turning it off and on?
• **Did** you **try** restarting it from the settings menu?
We would like to send a technician to look at the machine. Could you tell us what time is suitable?
We can talk about a replacement when the technician checks the machine.
We are sorry again for the problems you had.
Best regards,
Federico Franchesa
Customer Service Representative, Zafus

4.3 We are sorry that …

B Read the email again and answer the questions.
1 What three things does Federico ask about?
2 When can they talk about replacing the machine?

Communicative grammar

> **ASKING QUESTIONS ABOUT THE PAST** → Grammar reference: page 108

Did you **try** turning it off and on?	**Yes**, I/you/he/she/it/we/they **did**.
Did the technician **check** the machine?	**No**, I/you/he/she/it/we/they **didn't**.
Did it **work** after you put more paper in?	
When **did** the machine **stop** working?	
What **did** the technician **do**?	
Where **did** you **buy** it?	

5 Put the words in bold in the correct order.
1 **you did try** restarting it?
_____
2 **did the phone when stop** working?
_____
4 **did what the technician** say?
_____
5 **did where send you** the delivery?
_____

Teacher's resources: extra activities

→ **page 99** See Pronunciation bank: 'th' as /θ/ and /ð/

Writing

6 Complete the sentences with the phrases in the box.

| are sorry again | are sorry that | can talk about |
| some more information | what time is | would like to |

1 We _____ your tablet didn't work.
2 Can we get _____ about the problem?
3 We _____ check the phone.
4 Could you tell us _____ suitable?
5 We _____ a replacement when our technician checks your phone.
6 We _____ for the problems you had.

7 Look at page 115 and read the complaint email. Then write a reply like the one in Exercise 4A. Follow these steps.
- Say sorry for the problem.
- Ask for more information and ask for details of the problem.
  - can / we / more information?
  - try / remove tape?
  - try / turn off and on again
- Say you want to send a technician to look at the washing machine.
- Ask for a good time to visit.
- Say when you can talk about a new machine.

Self-assessment I can reply in a simple way to an email of complaint.

4.4 > WORK SKILLS
Face-to-face complaints

Lesson outcome — Learners can say sorry in work-related contexts.

Lead-in 1 Work in pairs. Look at the pictures. What is each person complaining about?

a broken product   a software problem   the wrong amount

2 🔊 4.06 Listen and read the dialogues. Match them with the pictures in Exercise 1.

1 **Customer:** Sorry, this is too much. I only bought three. This is the price for four.
Sales Assistant: I'm very sorry about that. I'll just change it and print you a new one.
2 **Customer:** When I make a video call, people can't hear me.
Customer Service: Really? Did you check the microphone settings?
3 **Customer:** I bought this yesterday but when I took it out of the box, I saw the screen was damaged.
Sales Assistant: I'm very sorry. Can I have a look at it?

VIDEO 3 ▶ 4.4.1 Watch Part 1 of the video and answer the questions.
1 What is the problem?
2 The Sales Assistant asks about two solutions. What are they?
3 Did the customer try them?

4A ▶ 4.4.2 Watch Part 2 of the video. Tick (✓) the offers the assistant makes.

to contact the phone maker   to give the customer a different phone
to give the customer her money back   to order a new phone   to repair the phone

B Watch Part 2 again and answer the questions.
1 What offer does the customer choose?
2 Why does she choose it?

5 Match 1–4 with a–d and 5–8 with e–h.

1 Really? What's   a your money back.
2 Did you try   b the problem?
3 So, I can give you   c turning it off and on again?
4 You can choose   d a different phone.

5 Let me just check when   e we can get you a replacement.
6 I'll order   f on Wednesday.
7 You can collect it   g it now.
8 OK, I'll call you   h when it's ready for collection.

44

4.4 | Work skills: Face-to-face complaints

Speaking

> **RESPONDING TO A COMPLAINT**
>
> **Asking about the problem**
> How can I help you?
> What's the problem?
> Can/Could you tell me about the problem?
>
> **Suggesting solutions**
> Did you try turning it off and on again?
> Did you change the battery?
> Did you try reinstalling the app?
>
> **Making offers**
> I can/could give you your money back.
> You can/could choose a different phone.
> I can/could order a new one.
>
> **Making promises**
> I'll order a new one now.
> You can collect it on Friday.
> I'll call you when it's ready.

Teacher's resources: extra activities

6 Work in pairs.
Student A: Follow the steps below. Student B: Look at page 117.

Student A: Scenario 1
You bought a laptop yesterday. When you got home, the laptop didn't turn on. Take it back to the shop and explain the problem to the Sales Assistant (Student B).
Read the notes and think about what you can say.

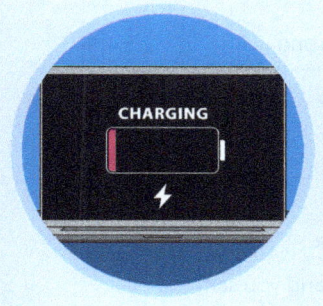

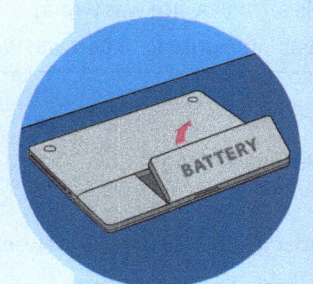

- Bought laptop yesterday.
- Didn't turn on.
- Tried charging it.
- Tried taking battery out and putting it back in.
- Didn't help.
- Listen to the Sales Assistant's options.
- Make a decision about what you prefer.

Student A: Scenario 2
You work in an electronics shop. A customer (Student B) will come in with a problem. Listen to his/her problem and use the notes to help him/her.
Read the notes and think about what you can say.

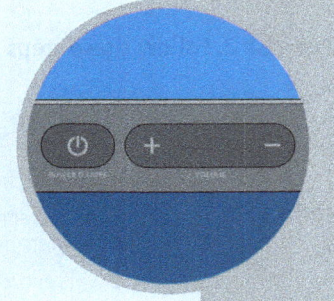

- Listen to the customer's problem.
- Ask the customer if he/she tried turning the phone off and on.
- Ask the customer if he/she tried cleaning the volume button.
- Tell the customer that you can:
    - give him/her his/her money back.
    - give him/her a different phone.
    - order a new one.
- Listen to the customer's choice.
- Tell the customer what you will do next.

Self-assessment I can say sorry in work-related contexts.

45

BUSINESS WORKSHOP

Can I help you?

Lesson outcome: Learners can make and receive simple phone calls about problems at work and understand and reply to emails of complaint.

Phone calls

1 Work in pairs. Roleplay a phone call.

Student A: Make the call. Read the information on this page.
Student B: Answer the call. Read the information on page 117.

Student A: Read the information. Then phone Student B.
- You work for Masacati Manufacturing.
- You bought a part for your machine from PTC Supplies.
- The part is broken.
- The order number is PTCS00785.
- Call PTC Supplies and ask them for a replacement.

Making a phone call

This is (your name) from (your company).

I/We bought ... yesterday / last week/month.

The ... is broken/late/lost.

There's a problem with ... .

Can you send us ... ?

Complaints

2 Read the email. Tick (✓) the problems the customer had.

a delivery was late   a part was broken   an invoice was wrong
someone sent the wrong replacement   the price for a part was wrong

Order number PTCS00785
S. Piancastelli<Simone.Piancastelli@Masacati.com>

Dear Sir/Madam,

I am writing to complain about our order (PTCS00785) from last week.

The first part you sent me was broken when it arrived. I phoned you and you sent me a replacement the next day. But I received part PNZ2654A and that's not what I ordered. And the replacement part is also broken.

Can you replace the part again please and use a different delivery company, or give us our money back?

I look forward to hearing from you.

Best regards,

Simone Piancastelli
Purchasing Manager, Masacati Manufacturing

Replying to a complaint

3 Write an email replying to the complaint in Exercise 2. Follow these steps and use the language in the box to help you.
- Say you are sorry about the problems.
- Ask a question about the delivery (e.g. box/arrive/damaged?).
- Ask a question about the replacement part (e.g. correct part number / PNZ2654H?).
- Offer to send the correct part.
- Offer to give the customer his/her money back because of the mistake.
- Say you are sorry again.

Replying to complaints

We are sorry that ...

Can we get some more information (about ...)?

We will send/give you ...

We would like to ...

We are sorry again for the problems you had.

Self-assessment: I can make and receive simple phone calls about problems at work and understand and reply to emails of complaint.

Office day to day   5

Unit overview

5.1 **What are you working on?**
Lesson outcome: Learners can talk in a simple way about their present activities at work.

Vocabulary: Word pairs
Communicative grammar: Talking about things happening now
Video: What are they doing?
Task: Writing about what people are doing now

5.2 **Are you free at two?**
Lesson outcome: Learners can make phone calls to arrange and postpone meetings.

Vocabulary: Word pairs
Listening: Organising meetings
Speaking: Arranging and postponing meetings

5.3 **Can we meet to discuss … ?**
Lesson outcome: Learners can write an email to arrange, accept or change a meeting.

Reading: Emails arranging, accepting or changing a meeting
Communicative grammar: Talking about future arrangements
Writing: An email arranging a meeting

5.4 **Work skills:** Can I ask a favour?
Lesson outcome: Learners can ask for a favour, offer help and respond to offers and requests for help.

Video: Can you help me?
Speaking: Doing favours

5.5 **Business workshop:** The meeting is at 3 p.m.
Lesson outcome: Learners can arrange, accept, cancel and postpone meetings by email and telephone.

Writing: An email to arrange a meeting to discuss a problem
Speaking: Postponing a meeting

| Review 5: p.91 | **Pronunciation:** 5.1 /ŋ/ and the Present Continuous 5.3 /ɪ/ and /iː/ p.100 | **Grammar reference:** 5.1 Talking about things happening now 5.3 Talking about future arrangements p.109 |

5.1 What are you working on?

Lesson outcome — Learners can talk in a simple way about their present activities at work.

Lead-in

1 Work in pairs. What do you do every day?

> have meetings   make phone calls   see suppliers
> send emails   visit clients   write reports   other

Vocabulary

Word pairs

> Designer   HR Manager
> Production Manager
> Purchaser   Sales Manager

2 🔊 5.01 Listen to Jane, Katie and Mark. What is each person's job? What do they do every day?

Jane – Sales Manager – go to meetings, ...

3 Cross out the word in each group that you **can't** use.
1 *have / prepare for / make / go to* a meeting
2 *make / receive / wait for / do* a phone call
3 *write* an email / a report / minutes / the telephone
4 *visit* a client / a colleague / a supplier / a presentation

4A Complete the sentences with words from Exercise 3.
1 The sales team **aren't visiting** a new _____ right now.
2 He**'s having** a(n) _____ with the client at the moment.
3 I**'m making** a(n) _____ now. Can we talk later?
4 They**'re not preparing** for the _____ at the moment.
5 We**'re visiting** a(n) _____ to check the order now.
6 I**'m writing** the _____ of yesterday's meeting right now.

T Teacher's resources: extra activities

B Match two sentences from Exercise 4A with the pictures.

Communicative grammar

> **TALKING ABOUT THINGS HAPPENING NOW**   ➡ Grammar reference: page 109
>
> I**'m (not) writ**ing the sales report now.
> You**'re (not) wait**ing for a phone call from a client at the moment.
> He/She**'s (not) travell**ing right now.
> We**'re (not) hav**ing a meeting right now.
> They**'re (not) visit**ing a supplier at the moment.

➡ **page 100** See Pronunciation bank: /ŋ/ and the Present Continuous

5 Complete the email with the phrases in the box.

> are visiting   'm not working
> 'm preparing   'm waiting
> 's travelling

Hi Susan,
Thanks for helping when I'm on holiday next week. There are a few important things I need to tell you before I go.
The board meeting is on Monday. I ¹_____ for it now. I ²_____ for an email from John with the presentation slides.
All of the sales team ³_____ clients at the moment so please ask them to send you their client reports next week.
Can you remind Sandra to do her report on Monday? She ⁴_____ at the moment and doesn't have access to email.
I ⁵_____ in the office today, so can you ask me questions tomorrow when I see you?
Thanks again!
Best wishes,
Tom

5.1 What are you working on?

6A Write sentences to describe what's happening in the pictures.

1 (write / email)
  I'm writing an email.

2 (visit / client)
  They're visiting a client.

3 (have / meeting)
  _____

4 (travel / for work)
  _____

5 (make / phone call)
  _____

6 (wait for / phone call)
  _____

7 (write / minutes)
  _____

8 (prepare for / meeting)
  _____

B Make the sentences in Exercise 6A negative.
I'm not writing an email.

Teacher's resources: extra activities

VIDEO

7A ▶ 5.1.1 Watch Part 1 of the video. Tick (✓) the person who talks about each of the activities.

Who:	Keir	Maria	Beata	Mo
is printing some documents?				
is waiting for a phone call?				
is writing invoices?				
is preparing a report?				

B Watch Part 2 of the video. Complete the sentences with words from the video.

1 Megan _____ a client.
2 Riaz _____ phone call to a client.
3 Jenny _____ invoices.
4 John _____ a sales report.

> TASK

8A Write sentences to describe what you think your colleagues, friends and people in your family are doing right now.

B Work in pairs. Read your sentences to your partner. If you know the person, do you agree?

Self-assessment I can talk in a simple way about my present activities at work.

5.2 Are you free at two?

Lesson outcome — Learners can make phone calls to arrange and postpone meetings.

Lead-in

1 Tick (✓) the people you have meetings with.

> colleagues   classmates   clients   my manager   my team   suppliers   teachers   other

2 Work in pairs. What do you talk about with the people in Exercise 1?

> contracts   costs   deadlines   delivery dates   payments
> projects   schedules   shipping   tests   other

Vocabulary — Word pairs

3A 🔊 5.02   Match 1–8 with a–h. Then listen and check.

1. Can we arrange a meeting with the client next week?
2. Did you talk to Chris?
3. What did you talk about in the meeting?
4. Sorry, but I need to cancel the meeting today.
5. How many different models do you have?
6. Can we postpone the meeting until next week?
7. What is the best thing about your products?
8. Do you know the date of the product launch?

a. No, I didn't. I need to speak to him tomorrow.
b. We checked the product specifications.
c. I think it's the 22nd of May.
d. We have twenty-five models in our product range.
e. We have very high product quality.
f. OK. I'll email Sandra and tell her.
g. Sure. I'm free on Wednesday.
h. Yes. Can we have it on Monday?

B Complete each spidergram with words from Exercise 3A.

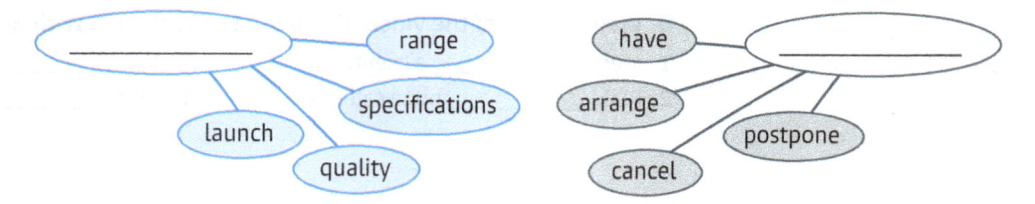

- _____ : range, specifications, launch, quality
- have, arrange, cancel, postpone : _____

Teacher's resources: extra activities

Listening — Organising meetings

4A 🔊 5.03   Listen to three phone calls. Who does each caller want to have a meeting with?

Who wants to have a meeting with ...	Phone call 1	Phone call 2	Phone call 3
a customer?			
a colleague?			
a supplier?			

5.2 Are you free at two?

B Listen to the phone calls again. Choose the correct option.

Phone call 1
1 The caller is calling to ____ .
   a arrange a meeting   b postpone a meeting   c cancel a meeting
2 The meeting is about ____ .
   a a product launch   b new product specifications   c the price of a new product
3 The meeting is ____ .
   a this afternoon   b tomorrow morning   c tomorrow afternoon

Phone call 2
4 The caller is calling to ____ .
   a arrange a meeting   b postpone a meeting   c cancel a meeting
5 The meeting is about ____ .
   a product prices   b the company's product range   c the product quality
6 The meeting is at ____ .
   a 2 p.m. on the 18th   b 3 p.m. on the 18th   c 2 p.m. on the 19th

Phone call 3
7 The caller is calling to ____ .
   a arrange a meeting   b postpone a meeting   c cancel a meeting
8 The meeting is about ____ .
   a a new order   b a reorder   c a return
9 The meeting is in the ____ .
   a morning on the 15th   b afternoon on the 18th   c morning on the 19th

5A 🔊 5.04 Complete the dialogue with the phrases in the box. Then listen and check.

can't do	free on
I'm busy	just check
see you	we arrange
we do	you free

A: Hello. Travelli. Marco Travelli speaking.
B: Hi, Marco. This is Dianne Grant at Malladi Tech here.
A: Hello, Dianne. How are you?
B: I'm good, thanks. Listen, we have a new product range. Can ¹_____ a meeting to talk about it?
A: Yes. That would be great.
B: Great. Are ²_____ on Monday?
A: Let me ³_____ . Sorry, ⁴_____ on Monday. I'm ⁵_____ Tuesday morning.
B: Oh. I ⁶_____ Tuesday. Can ⁷_____ Wednesday morning?
A: Yes, that's fine. I'll ⁸_____ then.
B: Great, see you on Wednesday. Bye.
A: Bye.

B Work in pairs. Practise the dialogue with your partner.

Speaking

6 Work in new pairs. Take turns being Student A and Student B.

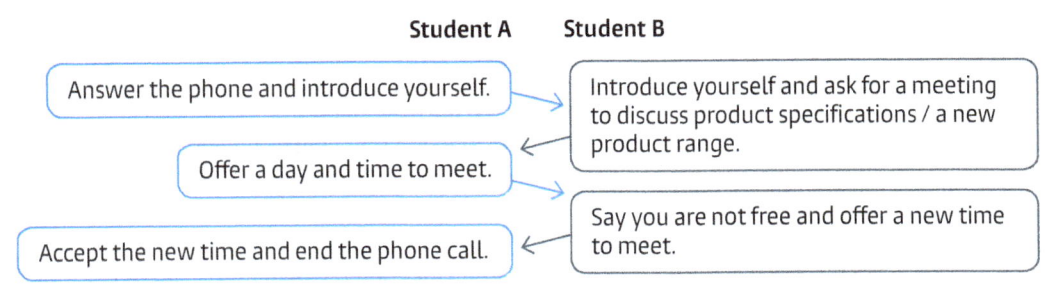

Student A — Answer the phone and introduce yourself.
Student B — Introduce yourself and ask for a meeting to discuss product specifications / a new product range.
Student A — Offer a day and time to meet.
Student B — Say you are not free and offer a new time to meet.
Student A — Accept the new time and end the phone call.

7 Work in pairs.
Student A: Look at page 116. Student B: Look at page 117.

Self-assessment
I can make phone calls to arrange and postpone meetings.

5.3 Can we meet to discuss … ?

Lesson outcome — Learners can write an email to arrange, accept or change a meeting.

Lead-in 1A Work in pairs. Which words from the box are in the pictures?

> a contract   a document
> a report   a spreadsheet
> an agenda   an invoice
> meeting minutes   notes
> presentation slides

B Which things in Exercise 1A do you often send as email attachments? What other things do you send?

Reading 2A Read the emails and put them in the correct order.

A
Hi Melissa,
I'm really sorry but I need to cancel our meeting tomorrow. We're **having** an emergency team meeting.
Are you working from home today? Can I call you after you talk to the client?
Best,
Sarah

B
Hi Melissa,
Here's a copy of the presentation slides for the clients **we're meeting** next week. Please find them attached.
Can we arrange a meeting before the presentation? I'd like to discuss the key points.
I'm not working in the office tomorrow so can we meet on Thursday? After lunch?
Thanks,
Sarah

C
Hi Sarah,
Thanks for the presentation slides. They are very good. **I'm talking** to the client tomorrow morning so it's fine to meet on Thursday afternoon. I'll see you then.
_____ ,
Melissa

> Three informal ways to end an email are:
> *Best regards,*
> *Thanks,*
> *Best,*
> We use them in the same way.

B Complete email c with the phrase from the box you prefer.

3 Read the emails in the correct order. Answer the questions with *Sarah*, *Melissa* or *both*.
Who …
1 prepared the presentation slides? ____Sarah____
2 asks for a meeting? _____
3 likes the presentation slides? _____
4 asks to change the meeting? _____
5 has a problem in their team? _____
6 doesn't always work in the office? _____

Communicative grammar

> **TALKING ABOUT FUTURE ARRANGEMENTS** → Grammar reference: page 109
>
> I'**m starting** a new job next month.
> You/We/They'**re meeting** the client next week.
> He/She'**s working** from home on Friday.
>
> I'**m not writing** the meeting minutes.
> You/We/They **aren't meeting** the client until next week.
> He/She **isn't working** in the office tomorrow.
>
> **Are** we/you/they **meeting** the client next week?
> **Is** he/she **working** in the office on Friday?

T Teacher's resources: extra activities

→ page 100 See Pronunciation bank: /ɪ/ and /iː/

5.3 Can we meet to discuss … ?

4A Choose the correct words.

Project meeting
Tim Moralis
t.moralis@webbertaylor.com

Hi Kiesha,

As you know, we ¹*'re starting / 's starting* a new project next month. I'd like to talk about the team roles with you. Can we arrange a meeting to discuss this?

I ²*'re not working / 'm not working* in the office tomorrow but I'm free on Wednesday.
³*Is you working / Are you working* in the office on Wednesday? Can we meet in the morning? At 9 a.m.?

Best regards,

Tim

B Complete the email with the correct form of the words in brackets.

Re: Project meeting
Kiesha Holongi
k.holongi@webbertaylor.com

Hi Tim,

I can meet on Wednesday at 9 a.m. but I ¹_____ (meet) some clients at 11 a.m. on Wednesday morning so we need to finish by 11 a.m. Then I ²_____ (visit) a supplier in the afternoon but will be back in the office at 3 p.m. if we need to talk more.
³_____ (you / work) from home tomorrow? If you prefer, we can do a video call.

Best,
Kiesha

C Complete the email with the correct form of the words in the box.

> not work   talk   visit   work

Re: Project meeting
Tim Moralis
t.moralis@webbertaylor.com

Hi Kiesha,

I'm sorry but I can't do our meeting tomorrow morning. Some of our team ¹_____ next week so I need to speak to them, and then I ²_____ to the HR team from 10 a.m. to 1 p.m. about some new staff. I'm not free later because I ³_____ a customer at 4 p.m. and I'm busy on Thursday. I ⁴_____ in the office all day on Friday so we can meet then.

Thanks,
Tim

Writing

5 Match 1–6 with a–f.

1 **I'm free** on Monday.
2 **I'm not free** on Monday.
3 **I'm really sorry but I need to cancel** our meeting.
4 **Can we arrange a meeting** on Monday?
5 **I'd like to talk about** the presentation.
6 **Please find** the presentation slides **attached**.

a **I'm sorry but I can't do** our meeting.
b **I'd like to discuss** the presentation.
c **Can we meet** on Monday?
d **Here's** a copy of the presentation slides.
e **I'm busy** on Monday.
f **I can meet** on Monday.

6A You are working with a colleague on a project. Write an email to him/her like the one in Exercise 4A.

- Ask to meet him/her to talk about the project.
- Explain why you want to meet him/her.
- Suggest a day and time to meet.

B Work in pairs. Exchange emails with your partner. Read your partner's email and write a reply like the one in Exercise 4B. Say you will come to the meeting on the day and time he/she suggested.

C Exchange emails with your partner. Read your partner's email and write another reply like the one in Exercise 4C. Explain you need to cancel the meeting. Give a reason and suggest a new day and time.

Self-assessment   I can write an email to arrange, accept or change a meeting.

5.4 WORK SKILLS
Can I ask a favour?

Lesson outcome — Learners can ask for a favour, offer help and respond to offers and requests for help.

Lead-in 1 Who can you ask these questions?

> a colleague   the IT team   your manager   other

1 Can you look at my computer? I can't send emails. *a colleague, …*
2 I can't find my copy of the budget report. Do you know where it is?
3 Can you help me finish this report?
4 Can I leave early today? My daughter's not well.
5 Do you know Anna's email address?

2 🔊 5.05 Put the sentences in the correct order. Then listen and check.

Conversation 1
a OK. Found it. Thanks. ____
b Oh … it's in the 'product descriptions' folder. ____
c Sorry, Paul, can I ask a favour? _1_
d Sure, Tony. How can I help? ____
e I can't find the presentation we're working on. Where did you save it? ____

Conversation 2
a OK, thanks. ____
b I'm looking for Viktor Dorret's contact details. Do you have them? ____
c Monika, do you have a minute? ____
d Just a minute. Here they are. I'll email them to you. ____
e Yes, sure. How can I help? ____

VIDEO 3A ▶ 5.4.1 Watch the video without sound. Do Martin, Jack and Andrea ask for help or offer help?

▶ Martin   ▶ Jack   ▶ Andrea

B Watch the video with sound. Choose the correct option.

1 Why does Martin need to leave early?
  a He is not well.
  b He wants to work from home.
  c His daughter is not well.
2 What does Yumiko want to know?
  a If Martin will be at work tomorrow.
  b If Martin can work from home.
  c If Martin finished the report.
3 Why does Jack offer to help Paulo?
  a Paulo can't use the photocopier.
  b Jack wants to use the photocopier.
  c Paulo asks him for help.

4 What does Paulo need help with?
  a Putting paper in the photocopier.
  b Sending a document from his computer.
  c Changing the ink in the photocopier.
5 Why does Andrea need help?
  a She doesn't know how to do the task.
  b Her computer doesn't work.
  c She has problems with her deadline.
6 Why can't Rachel help her?
  a She needs to finish some presentation slides.
  b She needs to finish a report.
  c She has a meeting.

4 Work in pairs. Are these problems common at your workplace or place of study?

5.4 Work skills: Can I ask a favour?

5A 🔊 5.06 Listen and complete the dialogue.

Yumiko: Hi, Martin. Do you need something?
Martin: Hi, Yumiko. Yes, could I ask a ¹_____?
Yumiko: Go on.
Martin: My daughter is not well and I need to pick her up from school. ²_____ I leave early?
Yumiko: ³_____ you work from home?
Martin: Yes. I think I can.
Yumiko: ⁴_____ . That's OK. I ⁵_____ see you tomorrow. I hope your daughter feels better.
Martin: Thanks, Yumiko. I'm sure she will.

B Work in pairs. Practise the dialogue in Exercise 5A.

Speaking

> **DOING FAVOURS**
>
> **Asking for help**
> Can/Could you help me?
> Can/Could I ask you for some help?
> Can/Could I ask a favour?
>
> **Offering help**
> Can I help you?
> Do you need some help with the report?
>
> **Agreeing to help**
> That's no problem.
> Yes, sure.
>
> **Accepting help**
> Yes, please.
> Thanks. That would be great.
>
> **Refusing to help**
> I'm really sorry but I'm too busy.
> I'm afraid I can't help you because I'm working on this presentation.
>
> **Refusing help**
> No, thanks.
> No, I'm fine. Thanks.
>
> **Suggesting someone else who can help**
> You could ask Jessica.
> Maybe Zach can help.
> Why don't you ask Richard?

T Teacher's resources: extra activities

6 Work in pairs. Make conversations.

Asking for help
- You have one of the problems below. Ask your partner for help.
  A: Could I ask a favour?
  B: Yes, sure.
  A: I'm having problems writing this report. Can you … ?

Offering help
- You can see your partner has one of the problems below. Offer to help.
  A: Are you OK?
  B: No, I can't open this document.
  A: Can I help you?

'I can't find a file I need to work on.'
'I need help writing a report.'
'I need to know someone's phone number.'
'I need to leave work early.'
'My computer doesn't work.'

Self-assessment — I can ask for a favour, offer help and respond to offers and requests for help.

BUSINESS WORKSHOP

The meeting is at 3 p.m.

Lesson outcome: Learners can arrange, accept, cancel and postpone meetings by email and telephone.

Arranging a meeting

1 Which sentences (1–8) can you use in an email to <u>arrange</u> a meeting? Which can you use in an email to <u>agree to</u> a meeting? And which sentences are from other types of emails?

To arrange a meeting: _____   To agree to a meeting: _____   Other: *1,* _____

1 I am writing to complain about my invoice.
2 I can meet on Monday. I'll see you then.
3 Can we meet to discuss the problem?
4 We are sorry that your invoice was wrong.
5 Yes, I'm free at 10 o'clock.
6 Are you free at 10 o'clock tomorrow?
7 Can we get some more information about the problem?
8 Can we arrange a meeting to talk about the project?

2 You need to meet your colleague to discuss a problem with a project. Write an email to arrange a meeting.
- Tell your colleague you want to meet.
- Say why you want to meet.
- Suggest a day and time to meet.

3 Work in pairs. Exchange emails with your partner. Read your partner's email and write a reply. Say you can come to the meeting on the day and time he/she suggested.

Postponing a meeting

4 Match the reasons for postponing a meeting (1–4) with the requests (a–d).

1 My son's not well so I need to pick him up from school early this afternoon.
2 John is not well today and can't come to the office so I need to do his work.
3 A machine broke and I need to go to the factory.
4 A client is thinking about changing supplier and I want to visit them.

a Could you email me a PDF of our complete product range?
b Could you call the machine supplier and order a new part?
c I'm meeting some new clients at 3 p.m. Can you meet them for me?
d Can you tell Jane I can't come to the meeting later because I have a lot of things to do?

5A Work in pairs. Roleplay a phone call.

Student A:
- You need to change the day/time of the meeting you arranged in Exercises 2/3.
- Call your colleague to postpone the meeting.
- Ask him/her a favour.
- Use an idea from Exercise 4 or one of your own.

Student B:
- Answer Student A's call.
- Say it's not a problem to change the day/time of the meeting you arranged in Exercises 2/3.
- Suggest an alternative time to meet.
- Agree to help when he/she asks for a favour.

A: Hello … This is … at … speaking. How can I help you?
B: Hi … This is … I'm sorry but I can't do our meeting. My son's not well so I need to pick him up from school early this afternoon. Can we … ?

B Change roles and postpone the other meeting you arranged by email.

Self-assessment: I can arrange, accept, cancel and postpone meetings by email and telephone.

An office move 6

Unit overview

6.1 **It's cheaper and better**
Lesson outcome: Learners can compare two options.

Vocabulary: Descriptions
Communicative grammar: Comparing two things
Video: An office move
Task: Choosing a warehouse

6.2 **Which is better?**
Lesson outcome: Learners can explain why they chose a specific offer.

Vocabulary: Orders
Speaking and reading: Supplier quotes
Writing: Describing different options

6.3 **Which is the best?**
Lesson outcome: Learners can write an email recommending a service and giving reasons.

Reading: An email about changing a mobile phone contract
Communicative grammar: Making proposals with *if*
Writing: An email comparing two offers

6.4 **Work skills:** As you can see on the slide, …
Lesson outcome: Learners can describe tables and graphs.

Video: A presentation about office equipment
Speaking: Talking about presentation slides

6.5 **Business workshop:** The office move
Lesson outcome: Learners can compare different options and present the best.

Reading: An email from the boss
Writing and speaking: Comparing two offices
Speaking: Presenting your choice

Review 6: p.92 | Pronunciation: 6.1 The vowel /ə/ 6.3 /æ/ and /ʌ/ p.101 | Grammar reference: 6.1 Comparing two things 6.2 *good – better – best/bad – worse – worst* 6.3 Making proposals with *if* p.110

6.1 It's cheaper and better

Lesson outcome | Learners can compare two options.

Lead-in **1A** Which pair is wrong?

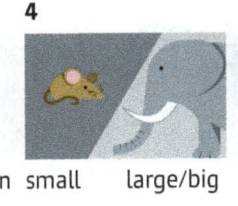

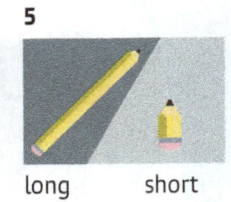

1	2	3	4	5	6
dark / light	noisy / quiet	old-fashioned / modern	small / large-big	long / short	cheap / expensive

B Which words describe your office/classroom?

Vocabulary Descriptions

2A Read the adverts and look at the words in bold. Match pictures A and B with the adverts.

▶ **THE MARSHALLS**

Is it **difficult** to park near your city-centre office?

This new business park is in **quiet** green countryside just 20 kilometres from the city. It has 15,000 m² of offices in a **spacious**, **modern** building and car park space for 3,000 cars. Bus stops and a train station are just a **short** fifteen-minute walk away.

Rents at the business park start at €46,000 a year.

▶ **AZTEC HOUSE**

Large offices are always **far** from the city centre or **expensive**, right?

This 25,000 m² office building is a **traditional** warehouse in the **busy** centre of the city. We are **close** to bars, restaurants and shops, and three train stations are not a **long** walk away – just five minutes – so your staff will have an **easy** journey.

Office rents are from €54,000 a year.

B Match the adjectives in bold in the adverts with their *comparative forms* in Exercise 2C.
difficult – more difficult

C Choose the correct option.
1 Aztec House is in a **quiet**er / **busi**er area than the Marshalls.
2 The walk to public transport from Aztec House is **short**er / **long**er than from the Marshalls.
3 Travel to the city is **easi**er / **more** difficult from the Marshalls.
4 Aztec House is **more** traditional / **more** modern than the Marshalls.
5 The Marshalls is **more** spacious / **small**er than Aztec House.
6 The Marshalls is **close**r / **further** than Aztec House *to* / *from* the city centre.
7 Rent at the Marshalls is **more** expensive / **cheap**er than at Aztec House.

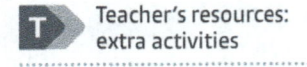

Teacher's resources: extra activities

Communicative grammar

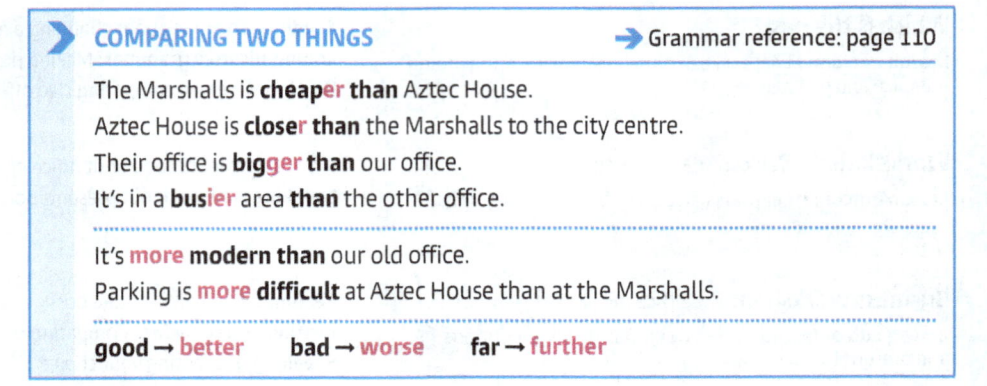

▶ **COMPARING TWO THINGS** → Grammar reference: page 110

The Marshalls is **cheap**er **than** Aztec House.
Aztec House is **close**r **than** the Marshalls to the city centre.
Their office is **bigg**er **than** our office.
It's in a **busi**er area **than** the other office.

It's **more** modern **than** our old office.
Parking is **more** difficult at Aztec House than at the Marshalls.

good → better   bad → worse   far → further

→ **page 101** See Pronunciation bank: The vowel /ə/

6.1 It's cheaper and better

3A Put the words in the correct order.
1 is / This office / than / more expensive / our old office.
   _____
2 Parking here / is easier / at our old office. / than
   _____
3 more modern / is / than / This building / that building.
   _____
4 bigger / It's / our old office. / than
   _____
5 darker / The building's / than / our old office.
   _____

B Complete the sentences with the correct form of the word in brackets.
1 We moved to a _more traditional_ (traditional) building in a _____ (quiet) area.
2 His office is _____ (close) to the station than my office.
3 The journey to my new office is _____ (long) than to my old office.
4 The conference was _____ (busy) than last year.
5 We need to move to a _____ (large) office than we have now.
6 The journey is _____ (short) by car.

Teacher's resources: extra activities

VIDEO

4A ▶ 6.1.1 Watch three people talking about an office move. Tick (✓) the things they talk about.

| bus stop   canteen   car park   distance from the city centre |
| distance from the train station   journey time   rent |

Comparisons with _more_ + noun
It has more parking spaces than city-centre offices have.

B Watch the video again and complete the table.

	Tim	Eleonora	Simon
The old office was ...	¹q_uieter_____	4 _____ , 5 _____	
The new office is ...	²l_____ , ³ _more_ m_____	6 _____ , 7 _____	8 _____
The canteen at the new office is ...	⁹s_____	10 _____	11 _____ , 12 _____

▶ TASK

5A Work in pairs. Follow these steps.
- You work for MacMurphy, a manufacturing company.
- Your company is looking for a new warehouse.
- Read the information about two warehouses and compare the two options.

	Wilson Lane	Leadson Road
Distance to factory	7 km	5 km
Space	25,000 m²	17,000 m²
Truck parking	9	6
Loading bays	5	4
Rent (per year)	€56,000	€49,000

Wilson Lane is larger than Leadson Road.

B Choose which warehouse to rent.
The perfect warehouse:
- is close to your factory.
- is 20,000 m² or bigger.
- can park six trucks or more.
- has six loading bays.
- is cheaper than €50,000 per year to rent.

Wilson Lane is further from the factory, but it's bigger.

Self-assessment I can compare two options. 😊 ☹

6.2 Which is better?

Lesson outcome — Learners can explain why they chose a specific offer.

Lead-in 1 Which of these do you buy a) in person b) online?

FURNITURE   IT EQUIPMENT   CLOTHES   FOOD AND DRINK   ENTERTAINMENT   GIFTS

I never buy clothes online. I always go to a shop!
I bought a gift for my friend Susan online yesterday, but …

Vocabulary   **Orders**

2 Look at the table. Which category in Exercise 1 does it match?

Quote for computer screens and laptops		
Product name:	27fw 68.58 cm (27") Ultraslim Full-HD IPS	NTBK E5420 11.6" LED
Unit price:	£169	£380
Number of units*:	10 screens	15 laptops
Delivery time:	30 days from order	10 days from order
Payment terms:	30 days from date of invoice by bank transfer	
Total price:	£1,690	£5,700
	£7,390	
***Minimum order** for free delivery: £500		

3 Match sentences 1–4 with some of the words in bold in Exercise 2.
1 Pay us £7,390 for 10 screens and 15 laptops. *total price*
2 We deliver the product for free on orders over £500.
3 Pay us no later than 30 days after we send you the invoice.
4 One screen costs £169.
5 This document tells you our price for the products we sell.

4 Look at the table in Exercise 2 again and complete the sentences with some of the words in bold.
1 The _____ are the same for both the laptops and the screens.
2 The _____ for the laptops is shorter.
3 The laptop's _____ is NTBK E5420 11.6" LED.
4 The _____ for ten screens is £1,690.
5 The _____ for the screens is £169 and £380 for the laptops.

Teacher's resources: extra activities

Speaking and reading   **Supplier quotes**

5A Work in groups of four. Morgan Whitaker wants to buy new chairs for its meeting rooms. They asked three suppliers to send them a quote.

Student A: Look at page 114. **Student B:** Look at page 118. **Student C:** Look at page 120.
Student D: Look at the table in Exercise 5B on page 61. Write the questions you need to ask to complete it. Check your questions with the ones on page 116.

6.2 Which is better?

B Student D: Ask Students A–C your questions and complete the table.

	The Work Furniture Specialist	Brench Office Supplies	Winners Office Supplies
Product name			
Unit price			
Minimum order			
Delivery time			
Payment terms			

C Work in groups and compare the three quotes. Which things are better and which things are worse?

I prefer the Soldero meeting chair because it's cheaper!
I think The Work Furniture Specialist is better because of the delivery time.

6 Complete the email with the company names from Exercise 5B.

Hi Paulo,

Thanks for sending me the quotes.

I think [1]_____ is the best quote. I know the chairs are more expensive than the others, but they look more comfortable.

I know [2]_____ are cheaper, but I think they'll have the worst quality. Also, the delivery time is longer than the other suppliers.

I like the offer from [3]_____ , but the minimum order is larger than the others. We only need sixteen chairs and I don't want to order twenty.

Because we can order sixteen from [4]_____ , it's cheaper and more practical to buy from them.

Let me know if you need further information.

Best,
Milo

GOOD – BETTER – BEST / BAD – WORSE – WORST

➡ Grammar reference: page 110

The Work Furniture Specialist's quote is **good**.
The Work Furniture Specialist's quote is **better than** Brench's and Winners'.
The Work Furniture Specialist's quote is **the best**.

Winners' quote is **bad**.
Winners' quote is **worse than** Brench's and The Work Furniture Specialist's.
Winners' quote is **the worst**.

Teacher's resources: extra activities

Writing

7A Your company wants to buy ten standing desks. Complete the sentences about the three different options.

	The Work Furniture Specialist	Brench Office Supplies	Winners Office Supplies
Product name	Willow Standing Desk	Fowler Standing Desk	Hersham Standing Desk
Unit price	$232	$440	$350
Minimum order	15	5	10
Delivery time	10 days	7 days	15 days
Payment terms	60 days	30 days	90 days

1 Winners Office Supplies is __*cheaper*__ __*than*__ Brench Office Supplies, but it's _____ _____ _____ The Work Furniture Specialist.
2 The Willow Standing Desk has _____ _____ price of the three.
3 Brench Office Supplies has a _____ minimum order than both Winners Office Supplies and The Work Furniture Specialist.
4 Winners Office Supplies' delivery time _____ _____ _____ Brench Office Supplies'.
5 The Work Furniture Specialist's payment terms _____ _____ _____ Brench Office Supplies'.

B Use the information in the table in Exercise 7A to write your own five sentences.

Self-assessment I can explain why I chose a specific offer.

6.3 Which is the best?

Lesson outcome — Learners can write an email recommending a service and giving reasons.

Lead-in

1A Which sentences are true for you?

1. I don't pay extra for calls in my country or to the USA.
2. I can send hundreds and hundreds of pictures and texts at no extra cost.
3. My contract is for twenty-four months.
4. I can choose the phone I want.
5. I don't pay much for my contract.

B Match the sentences in Exercise 1A with the phrases in the box.

> a wide range of phones   competitive prices   fixed-term contracts
> free national and international calls   unlimited data and texts

C Compare your phone provider with your partner's.

2 Complete the advert with words from Exercise 1B.

star
BUSINESS MEDIA SOLUTIONS

Our premium phone packages offer:
* Competitive ¹_____
* Fixed-term ²_____ of 12, 24 or 36 months
* Unlimited ³_____
* Free national and ⁴_____ calls
* A wide ⁵_____ of phones at the best prices

Contact us for more information on +44 20 7946 0724 or by email.

Reading

3A BDWN, a financial services company, wants a new mobile phone contract with Star. Read the email and complete the sentence.

Katia thinks the best package is 'Business _____ ' because it's _____ .

Re: Changes to phone contract
Katia
k.robinson@bdwn.fin.com

Hi Gemma,

Star, our mobile provider, are offering us two packages. Please see the attachment for more details. In summary:

- The 'Business standard' package will cost us $2,600 per month. **If** we **choose** this package, we**'ll have** a twenty-four-month contract. We'll get 3GB of free data per user, but it'll be slower than the other package. We'll also get unlimited texts and free national calls, but we'll pay 20 cents per minute for international calls.
- The 'Business plus' package will cost us $4,450 per month. **If** we **get** this package, we**'ll have** a twelve-month contract and we'll get unlimited data – faster than the other package – and unlimited texts and free calls. This includes international calls.

I think the 'Business standard' package is better for us because it's cheaper. We don't need the unlimited data or the international calls in the more expensive 'Business plus' package. **If** we **choose** 'Business standard', we**'ll save** a lot of money.

Let me know if you have any questions.

Thanks,
Katia

B Read the email again. Complete the table.

	BUSINESS STANDARD	BUSINESS PLUS
Price	$2,600	¹_____
Data	²_____	unlimited
Texts	unlimited	³_____
National calls	free	⁴_____
International calls	⁵_____	free

62

6.3 Which is the best?

Communicative grammar

> **MAKING PROPOSALS WITH *IF*** → Grammar reference: page 110
>
> **If** you **choose** the 'Business standard' package, it**'ll cost** $2,600 per month.
> **If** he **chooses** this package, he**'ll get** 3GB of free data per user.
> **If** we **take** the 'Business plus' package, it**'ll cost** $4,450 per month.
> **If** they **get** this package, they**'ll have** a twelve-month contract.

→ **page 101** See Pronunciation bank: /æ/ and /ʌ/

4A Complete the sentences with the correct form of the words in brackets.
1. If you _____ (buy) the standard package, you _____ (get) 3GB of data.
2. If she _____ (order) today, she _____ (save) money.
3. If we _____ (take) this package, it _____ (cost) more.
4. If they _____ (get) a bigger office, they _____ (have) more space.
5. If I _____ (sell) more, I _____ (make) more money.
6. If he _____ (have) faster internet, he _____ (receive) email attachments faster.

B Write proposals using *if* with the prompts.
1. you / choose the plus package / you / get unlimited data
   If *you choose the plus package, you'll get unlimited data* _____ .
2. we / take the standard package / we / have a twenty-four-month contract
   If _____ .
3. he / buy now / he / get better payment terms
   If _____ .
4. I / choose the standard package / save money
   If _____ .
5. they / order more / they / have a lower unit price
   If _____ .
6. she / change the order / the delivery time / be longer
   If _____ .

Teacher's resources: extra activities

Writing

5A Work with a partner. Look at the table in Exercise 5B. Match 1–4 with a–d.
1. I think Magnus 1 **is better because** it's   a cheaper.
2. I think AmuTel **is better because** it has   b a shorter contract.
3. I think Magnus 1 **is better because** we get   c faster.
4. I think we should choose AmuTel **because** it's   d free national and international calls.

B You are an Office Manager and have two offers for office phones and internet. Write an email like the one in Exercise 3A to the Managing Director.
- Use the information in the table.
- Compare the two offers.
- Include proposals with *if*.
- Explain which offer you prefer and why.

	AMUTEL	MAGNUS 1
Price	$4,300 per month	$6,000 per month
Speed	250GB per second	750GB per second
National calls	free	free
International calls	10 cents per minute	free
Contract	twelve months	twenty-four months

Self-assessment I can write an email recommending a service and giving reasons.

6.4 WORK SKILLS
As you can see on the slide, …

Lesson outcome — Learners can describe tables and graphs.

Lead-in 1A Complete the slides with the words in the box.

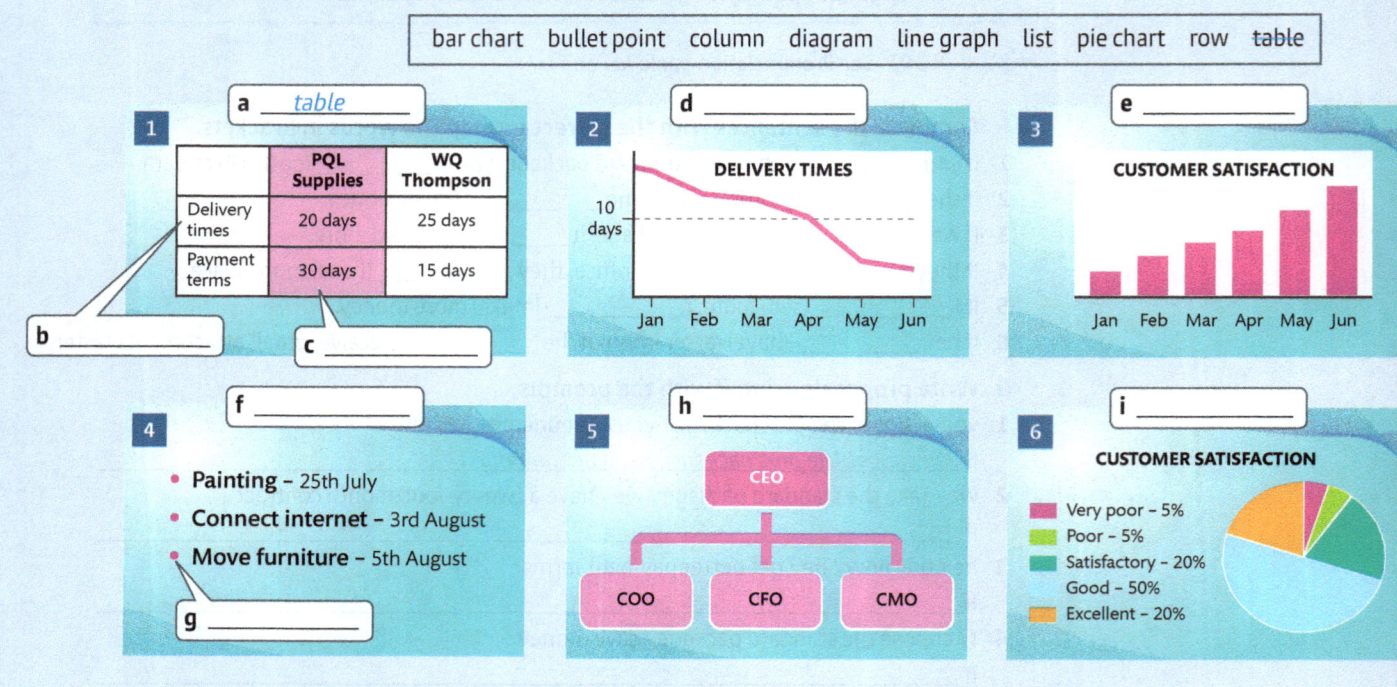

> bar chart   bullet point   column   diagram   line graph   list   pie chart   row   table

1 a _table_

	PQL Supplies	WQ Thompson
Delivery times	20 days	25 days
Payment terms	30 days	15 days

b _____   c _____

2 d _____
DELIVERY TIMES (10 days) Jan Feb Mar Apr May Jun

3 e _____
CUSTOMER SATISFACTION — Jan Feb Mar Apr May Jun

4 f _____
- Painting – 25th July
- Connect internet – 3rd August
- Move furniture – 5th August

g _____

5 h _____
CEO → COO, CFO, CMO

6 i _____
CUSTOMER SATISFACTION
- Very poor – 5%
- Poor – 5%
- Satisfactory – 20%
- Good – 50%
- Excellent – 20%

B Match the sentences (i–vi) with the slides (1–6) in Exercise 1A.

i The delivery times are now shorter than in January. Slide _2_
ii Unfortunately, we can't move to the new office until August. Slide ___
iii Three people report to the Chief Executive Officer. Slide ___
iv WQ Thompson's delivery times are longer than PQL Supplies'. Slide ___
v Customer satisfaction is higher now than in March. Slide ___
vi Ninety percent of our customers are satisfied with our service. Slide ___

VIDEO 2A ▶ 6.4.1 Watch the video. Which of these items are in the video?

> a bar chart   a bullet-pointed list   a diagram   a graph   a pie chart   a table

B Watch the video again. Are the sentences *true* (T) or *false* (F)?
1 The Sales Representative is selling laser and inkjet printers and photocopiers.
2 The Macinda is slower than the Zindex A320.
3 The Zindex can print fifteen pages per minute.
4 The Zindex's guarantee is shorter than the Macinda's guarantee.
5 If you buy the Macinda, you will pay more per copy.
6 If you buy twenty printers, you will get a 10 percent discount on them.

3 Match 1–7 with a–g.

1 As you can see from
2 This table shows you the three main
3 The second column is the Zindex A320
4 As you can see in the second row,
5 If you look at the third column, row three,
6 Row four of
7 Let's look

a differences between the two models.
b the Zindex is faster than the Macinda.
c the table shows the price of toner for the Zindex and ink for the Macinda.
d you will see that the Macinda's guarantee is longer.
e at the price, delivery time and payment terms.
f these bar charts, the Zindex A320 is the best laser printer/photocopier on the market.
g and the third column is the Macinda 360.

64

6.4 Work skills: As you can see on the slide, ...

Speaking

> **TALKING ABOUT PRESENTATION SLIDES**
>
> **Talking about slides**
> Now, let's look at customer satisfaction.
> This slide shows two bar charts.
> As you can see on the slide, sales of furniture were higher in Q1 than in Q2.
>
> **Talking about images, charts and tables**
> As you can see from the pie chart, we spend less on office supplies.
> If you look at the table, you can see that the sales are higher by 10 percent.
> If you look at the fourth row, you'll see that we spend more on rent.

T Teacher's resources: extra activities

4 🔊 6.01 Look at the bar chart and complete the text. Listen and check.

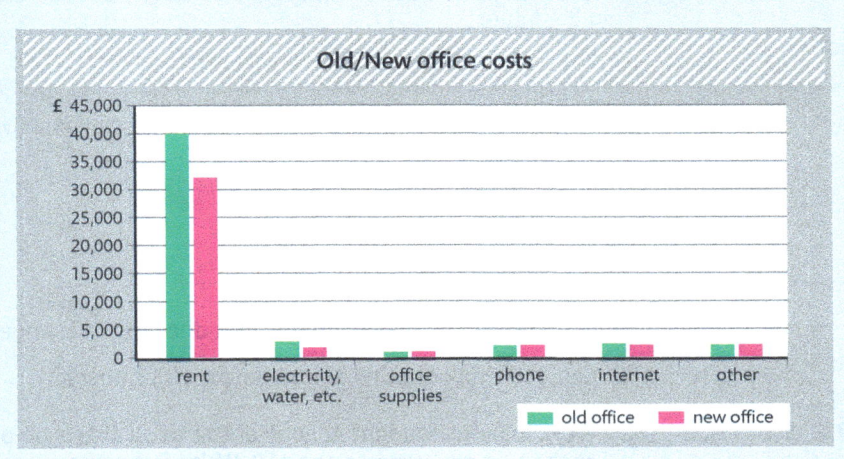

Old/New office costs — bar chart showing rent, electricity/water etc., office supplies, phone, internet, other (old office vs new office)

Now, ¹l _ _ 's look ²_ _ our office costs. This ³b _ _ c _ _ _ t ⁴s _ _ _ s the main differences in costs between the old office and the new office. As you ⁵c _ _ s _ _ , the rent of the new office is cheaper by £8,000. If you ⁶l _ _ k _ t the cost of electricity, water, etc., ⁷you'_ _ s _ _ that this cost is also lower. The cost of office supplies, for example paper, ink, pens and phones is the same, but we pay a little less for the internet. So in total we save about 15 percent per month on our new office.

5A Work in pairs.
  Student A: Look at page 122 and complete the description of your slide.
  Student B: Look at page 119 and complete the description of your slide.

B Work in pairs.
  Student A: Give a short presentation to your partner about the two internet providers. Use the slide with your presentation.
  Student B: Listen to your partner's description. Are the sentences true or false?
  1 The table shows the four main differences between Intranui Internet and Priomea Connect.
  2 Intranui Internet is cheaper than Priomea Connect.
  3 Intranui Internet's contract is longer than Priomea Connect's contract.

C Work in pairs.
  Student B: Give a short presentation to your partner about the customers in Europe and Africa. Use the slide with your presentation.
  Student A: Listen to your partner's description. Are the sentences true or false?
  1 The slide shows a bar chart of customers in Europe and Africa.
  2 The number of customers in Africa was lower in June than in January.
  3 May was a good month for Europe and Africa.

Self-assessment I can describe tables and graphs. 🙂 🙁

BUSINESS WORKSHOP

The office move

Lesson outcome: Learners can compare different options and present the best.

An email from the boss

1A Work in pairs. You and your colleague manage the office in a small company. You receive this email from the Managing Director. What does she want you to do?

Possible office move
Sandra
s.olson@fdw-consulting.com

Hi,

As you know, we're thinking about moving office. This one is very small for us. I'd like you to look for four or five possible offices for us.

For me, the perfect office:
- is a modern office in the city centre, but I'm happy to hear other ideas!
- needs space for all our employees – 22 people at the moment – and space for us to grow in the future.

I know a bigger office will be more expensive than this one, but we need to be careful with money! I think our maximum will be $2,500 per month.

We also need parking and fast internet. And we'll need a five-year contract or longer.

Did I forget anything?

Thanks,

Sandra

B Read the email again. What things does the office need?

C Can you think of other things a new office needs?

Choose an office

2A Work in pairs. Student A: Look at the two adverts on page 121. Student B: Look at the two adverts on page 119. Write five sentences comparing your two offices. Then choose which office you think your boss would prefer.

Berlin House is bigger than 1A Foster Street.

B Share your sentences with your partner and say which office you think your boss would prefer.

C Work together and compare the two offices you prefer. Choose <u>one</u> to present to your boss.

I think the Wordells is the best. It's in the city, and it's cheaper than 1A Foster Street …

Present your choice

3 🔊 6.02 Listen to a presentation. Complete the gaps with the words you hear.

Anna: So, we think 23 Beaker Street is the best option. ¹_____ a list of details about 23 Beaker Street. It's bigger than our office now, and it's close to the city centre. It's also close to a train station and a bus stop. They're about a five-minute walk.

However, ²_____ , it's not perfect because the car park is smaller and the internet is slower than what we have at the moment.

Tony: Now, ³_____ prices. The office costs $1,900 a month so it's more expensive than our office at the moment but cheaper than other offices in the city centre. If you look ⁴_____ , you will see that we can choose a five- or ten-year contract, so that's really good.

---

23 BEAKER STREET
- Bigger than our office now
- Close to city centre and transport
- Small car park
- Slow internet
- $1,900/month
- Five- or ten-year contract

4A Work in pairs. Compare the office you chose to Sandra's ideas in the email in Exercise 1A. Prepare a presentation about your choice. Prepare a slide with key information to show in your presentation.

B Present your office to another pair.

Self-assessment I can compare different options and present the best.

Procedures

7

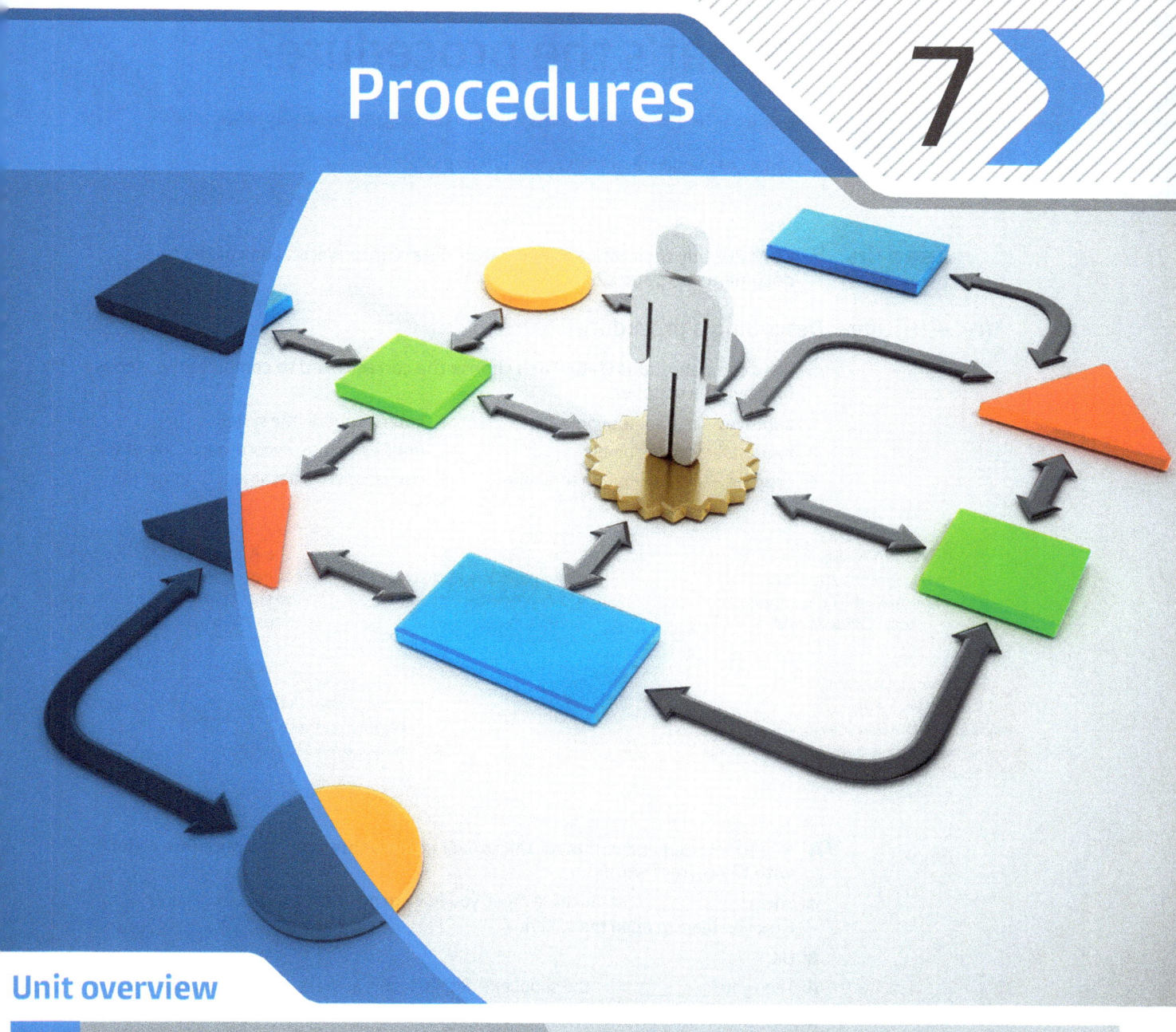

Unit overview

7.1	**What's the procedure?** **Lesson outcome:** Learners can understand and explain simple procedures.	**Vocabulary:** Describing a procedure **Communicative grammar:** Talking about obligation **Video:** Paying suppliers **Task:** Explaining a procedure
7.2	**Workflow** **Lesson outcome:** Learners can describe problems in a simple workflow.	**Vocabulary:** Descriptions **Reading and listening:** A workflow problem **Speaking:** Improving a workflow
7.3	**A manual** **Lesson outcome:** Learners can write a simple manual explaining a procedure.	**Reading:** A manual **Communicative grammar:** Instructions **Writing:** Instructions for creating an invoice
7.4	**Work skills:** Changing a workflow **Lesson outcome:** Learners can discuss workflows and ways of improving a workflow.	**Video:** A new workflow **Speaking:** Making and responding to suggestions
7.5	**Business workshop:** How can we improve it? **Lesson outcome:** Learners can discuss problems with a workflow and suggest improvements.	**Reading:** Identifying problems in a workflow **Speaking:** Discussing solutions; Responsibilities in a new workflow

Review 7: p.93 | **Pronunciation:** 7.2 /aɪ/ and /eɪ/ 7.3 /l/ and /r/ p.102 | **Grammar reference:** 7.1 Talking about obligation 7.3 Instructions p.110

7.1 What's the procedure?

Lesson outcome — Learners can understand and explain simple procedures.

Lead-in 1 KDTX PLC buy their office supplies from Total Office World. Look at the two documents on page 122.

Vocabulary Describing a procedure

2 Read the definitions (1–6). Then choose the correct word to complete the stages for paying a supplier.

1 **approves** – says something is OK
2 **requests** – asks for something
3 **supplies** – gives an item to someone
4 **enters** – puts in the system
5 **notifies** – tells someone about something
6 **issues** – gives a document to someone

- An Admin Assistant at KDTX creates a purchase order (PO) and emails it to the supplier, Total Office World.
- Total Office World [1]*supply / enter* the items and [2]*issue / request* an invoice.
- The Admin Assistant at KDTX [3]*notifies / enters* the invoice from the supplier on the system and sends the invoice for approval.
- The system [4]*approves / notifies* the manager that there is a new invoice.
- The manager [5]*approves / issues* the invoice.
- The Admin Assistant [6]*requests / notifies* payment of the invoice on the payment system.

3A 🔊 7.01 Listen and complete the conversation about issuing a purchase order with the correct words.

A: So, to [1]_____ a purchase order, you **have to go** into the payment system. First, you **have to open** the system.

B: OK.

A: Then you [2]_____ the supplier's details: name, address, etc. on the system.

B: Do I **have to do** that every time?

A: No, you don't. You can choose it from a list here. When you have the supplier's details, you enter the price here and the delivery date here. You can find the information on the contract.

B: And do I [3]_____ the supplier that the purchase order's ready?

A: No, you **don't have to do** that. The system notifies the supplier automatically by email.

B: OK, that's clear. What's next?

A: The supplier delivers the items and [4]_____ payment.

B: So they **have to tell** us to pay them. Right?

A: Yes, they [5]_____ an invoice with the purchase order number on it. We can't pay invoices without a purchase order number. You **have to check** the invoice against the purchase order. If it's correct, you can [6]_____ management approval. The manager [7]_____ the payment. And when they approve it, you can make the payment. But that's later. Do you want to try to create a purchase order?

B: Yes, please.

B Put the stages in the order they happen in the conversation in Exercise 3A.

a ___ supply goods/ complete work
b ___ issue invoice
c ___ approve payment
d ___ enter supplier on the system

T Teacher's resources: extra activities

68

7.1 What's the procedure?

Communicative grammar

> **TALKING ABOUT OBLIGATION** → Grammar reference: page 110
>
> \+ I/You/We/They **have to send** the invoice to the client.
> He/She **has to approve** payment.
>
> \- I/You/We/They **don't have to email** the supplier (because the system does it).
> He/She **doesn't have to email** the client (but he/she can do if he/she wants).
>
> ? **Do** I/you/we/they **have to approve** the payment?
> Yes, I/you/we/they **do**. / No, I/you/we/they **don't**.
> **Does** every invoice **have to have** the PO number on it?
> Yes it **does**. / No, it **doesn't**.

4 Complete the conversation with the correct form of *have to*.

A: I ¹_____ check for new contracts every day. When I issue a contract, I ²_____ send it to my manager.
B: Does your manager ³_____ approve all contracts?
A: Yes, she ⁴_____. Then I ⁵_____ send it to the supplier and they have to sign it within thirty days. The supplier ⁶_____ issue an invoice when they finish the work.
B: Does your manager ⁷_____ approve the invoice?
A No, she ⁸_____. But I ⁹_____ check the information on the invoice. I can then pay the supplier.

5 Write conversations using *have to*.

1. A: she / check for new contracts?
   B: Yes / She / check for new contracts / every day.

   Does she have to check for new contracts?
   Yes, she does. She has to check for new contracts every day.

2. A: you / approve contracts?
   B: Yes / I / approve all contracts.
   _____
   _____

3. A: he notify / suppliers / about the purchase order?
   B: No / he / notify the suppliers.
   _____
   _____

4. A: the purchase order number / be on the invoice?
   B: Yes / The purchase order number / be on all invoices.
   _____
   _____

Teacher's resources: extra activities

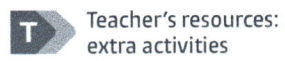

VIDEO

6A ▶ 7.1.1 Bernice is a Project Administrator in a large international company. Watch the video and tick (✓) the tasks she does.

a Check email for new contracts
b Create a purchase order
c Enter supplier details
d Notify manager about new purchase orders
e Approve purchase orders
f Send purchase order numbers to suppliers
g Include purchase order numbers on invoices
h Check invoices

B Watch again. Who/What does the tasks in Exercise 6A that Bernice <u>doesn't</u> do?

| an administrator | the manager | the supplier | the system |

C Make one sentence about Bernice using *have to* for each step in Exercise 6A.

TASK

7 Work in pairs.
Student A: Look at page 118 and read the information.
Student B: Look at page 121 and read the information.

Self-assessment

I can understand and explain simple procedures.

7.2 Workflow

Lesson outcome | Learners can describe problems in a simple workflow.

Lead-in **1A** Label the products on the webpage (1–8) with the words in the box.

> 5 HB pencils   12 black pens   100 brown envelopes   500 sheets of paper
> a printer ink cartridge   a ring binder   a stapler   headphones

OFFICE 2U DIRECT   5% discount on orders over $100   10% discount on orders over $200

| 1 _____ $4.75 | 2 _____ $6.20 | 3 _____ $3.80 | 4 _____ $5.20 |
| 5 _____ $17.50 | 6 _____ $7.40 | 7 _____ $4.75 | 8 _____ $22.00 |

B Work in pairs. How much does each order cost?
1. Eight packs of pens and twelve packs of pencils
2. Fifteen ring binders and ten staplers
3. Five printer ink cartridges, six packs of paper, twenty packs of envelopes and three sets of headphones

Vocabulary   Descriptions

2 Read the feedback from clients. Are they *happy* (H) or *unhappy* (U) with the service from Office2UDirect?

1. The Office2UDirect website is really **clear** – it's very easy to understand.   *H*
2. Office2UDirect are really **reliable**. They always have good-quality products and deliver quickly.
3. The products are **excellent** – great quality and good prices.
4. Their online order form is long and **complicated** – I couldn't understand it.
5. The delivery is very **efficient**. Packages always arrive on schedule.
6. The order process was **simple** and really easy to use.
7. Office2UDirect are totally **unreliable**. Late deliveries, incorrect invoices, …
8. The stapler was cheap but the quality was really **poor**. It didn't work. Don't buy it!

7.2 Workflow

3 Match 1–8 with a–h.

1. This website is really easy to read.
2. The products are not well made.
3. The delivery company delivers orders quickly.
4. The order form was simple.
5. They have excellent customer service.
6. The form needs lots of information.
7. The software stops working every week.
8. They always deliver on schedule.

a. I only needed five minutes to fill it in.
b. It's very complicated.
c. It's very clear.
d. It's really unreliable.
e. They're very efficient – it's usually only 24 hours.
f. They're really poor quality and often break.
g. They're always friendly when they answer the phone.
h. They're a reliable company.

Reading and listening

A workflow problem

4 Complete the workflow for Office2UDirect with the stages in the box.

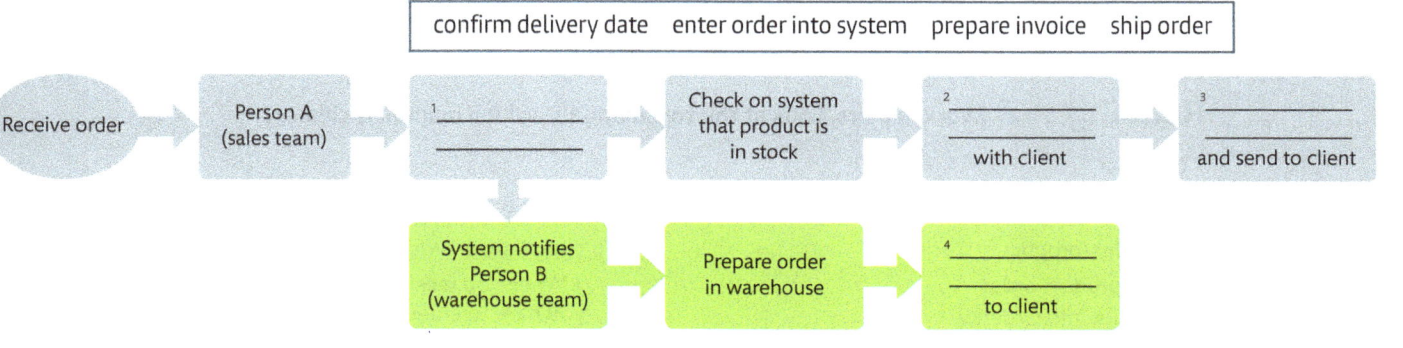

confirm delivery date   enter order into system   prepare invoice   ship order

Receive order → Person A (sales team) → 1 _____ → Check on system that product is in stock → 2 _____ with client → 3 _____ and send to client

System notifies Person B (warehouse team) → Prepare order in warehouse → 4 _____ to client

5 🔊 7.02 Listen to the meeting between the Sales Manager and the Warehouse Manager at Office2UDirect. Choose the correct option.

1. Office2UDirect are *only receiving complaints / receiving positive and negative comments* at the moment.
2. The sales department *always / never* check the inventory system when they receive an order.
3. The warehouse team *can / can't* always find the items they need for the orders.
4. The problems are usually with *big / small* orders.
5. The sales team don't check with the *warehouse / client* the number of items on the order.
6. The inventory system is *efficient / unreliable* because it only updates once a week.

➡ **page 102** See Pronunciation bank: /aɪ/ and /eɪ/

6 Match the problems (1–4) with the solutions (a–d).

1. Customers say our order form is complicated and difficult to fill in.
2. We get a lot of complaints about the poor quality of the CJH6039 stapler.
3. The sales team don't communicate with the warehouse team about shipping.
4. We only ship orders once a week. So delivery times vary between two and five days. Customers say we are unreliable.

a. I think we should stop selling it.
b. The warehouse team have to confirm shipment dates with the sales team.
c. Let's send them on Tuesdays and Thursdays.
d. We could change the design to make it simple.

Speaking

7A Work in pairs.
Student A: Look at page 120 and read the instructions.
Student B: Look at page 121 and read the instructions.

B Decide which solution from Exercise 7A you prefer.
I think we should …

Self-assessment I can describe problems in a simple workflow.

Teacher's resources: extra activities

7.3 A manual

Lesson outcome — Learners can write a simple manual explaining a procedure.

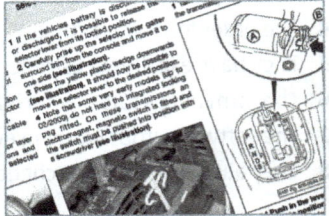

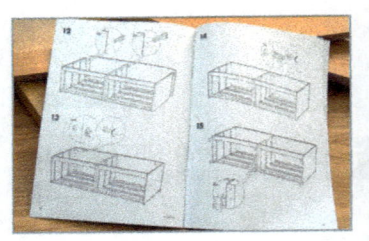

Lead-in 1A Work in pairs. What do you use manuals for?

| cars | computers | furniture | phones | software | other |

B Are they easy or difficult to use? Why?

Reading 2 Work in pairs. Look at the two manuals. Which manual is clearer?

Manual A

To complete an order (product in stock):
1 **Receive** the product order.
2 **Enter** the order into OrderKwik.
3 **Check** the inventory.
4 If the product is in stock, **organise** shipping.
5 **Confirm** the delivery date with the customer.
6 **Remember** to check the address.
7 **Prepare** the invoice for the customer.
8 **Send** the invoice by email.

Manual B

To complete an order (product in stock):

1 When you receive the order from the customer, first you have to enter it into the OrderKwik system.

2 If the product is available, ask your colleagues to ship it to the customer. Then you have to confirm the date of delivery with the customer. Don't forget to check the shipping address!

3 Next, you have to prepare the invoice for the customer and finally send it to him or her by email.

3 Read Manual A in Exercise 2. Are the sentences *true* (T) or *false* (F)? Correct the false sentences.
1 When the employee receives the order, he/she has to enter the order details.
2 Then, the employee has to check the product is available.
3 The employee doesn't have to organise shipping; this is automatic.
4 The employee has to contact the customer to confirm the delivery date.
5 Finally, the employee sends the invoice to the customer by post.

4 Look at Manual A again. Which statement is not true?
1 The instructions are short and simple.
2 The instructions are clear.
3 The instructions are in a logical order.
4 The instructions use words like 'when', 'first' and 'then'.
5 The instructions include all stages of the procedure.

Communicative grammar

> **INSTRUCTIONS** → Grammar reference: page 111
>
> **Send** the completed form by 20th April.
> **Don't send** bank details by email.
> **Check** all the customer details are correct.
> **Remember** to sign the document. / **Don't forget** to sign the document.

7.3 A manual

5A Choose the correct word to complete the instructions.

To create a new supplier:

a *Approve / Don't approve* the supplier's fee in the final box. ____
b Finally, *forget / don't forget* to press 'Save'. ____
c *Remember / Don't remember* to include the project details. ____
d *Check / Don't check* the supplier's information carefully before you continue. _3_
e *Complete / Don't complete* the supplier's information. ____
f *Click / Don't click* 'Create new supplier' on the system. ____

B Put the instructions in Exercise 5A into the correct order.

6 Complete the instructions with the verbs in the box. There may be more than one possible answer.

check click complete ~~download~~ forget phone remember send

To register for the conference:

1 ✓ _Download_ the registration form here.
2 ✓ _____ it with your first name, surname, date of birth and address.
3 ✓ _____ all the information is correct before you send us the form.
4 ✗ _____ your bank account details with the form. Email them separately.
5 ✗ _____ to add your electronic signature.
6 ✓ _____ here to submit the completed registration form.
7 ✓ _____ to send us an email with your travel details.
8 ✓ _____ or email us if you have any problems.

→ **page 102** See Pronunciation bank: /l/ and /r/

Teacher's resources: extra activities

Writing

7 Look at the highlighted information in this invoice. Use it to write a list of instructions for creating an invoice.

To prepare an invoice for a customer:
1 Write our company name and address in the top left-hand corner.

[Company Name]
[Company address]
[City, State, Zip]
[Phone]

INVOICE

INVOICE NUMBER	DATE
[123456]	5/1/2019

INVOICE TO

[Name]
[Company name]
[Street address]
[City, State, Zip]
[Phone]
[Email address]

DESCRIPTION	AMOUNT
Purchase order number: 78910	
Service fee	200.00
Labour hours @ $75/hr	375.00
New client discount	(50.00)
Tax (4.25% after discount)	22.31
Thank you for your business! **TOTAL**	547.31

Self-assessment: I can write a simple manual explaining a procedure.

7.4 ▶ WORK SKILLS
Changing a workflow

Lesson outcome — Learners can discuss workflows and ways of improving a workflow.

Lead-in

1 Put the tasks for new employees into a logical category in the table.

> ~~accept job offer~~   attend induction meetings   discuss tasks
> do health and safety training   do job-specific training   get a medical certificate
> give references   ~~meet colleagues~~   provide bank details
> send copies of qualifications and diplomas   sign a contract   tour the offices
> set up an email address

Before your first day	On your first day or after your first day
accept job offer	*meet colleagues*

2A 🔊 7.03 Listen to Laure talking about starting a new job. Tick (✓) the things in Exercise 1 she mentions.

B Listen again. Put the things she mentions in the correct order.

C What did Laure find a problem?

VIDEO 3A ▶ 7.4.1 Watch Part 1 of the video. Look at the workflow. Write down who is responsible for each stage: *Yumiko* (Y), *Human Resources* (HR), *New starter* (NS), *IT* or *Line Manager* (LM).

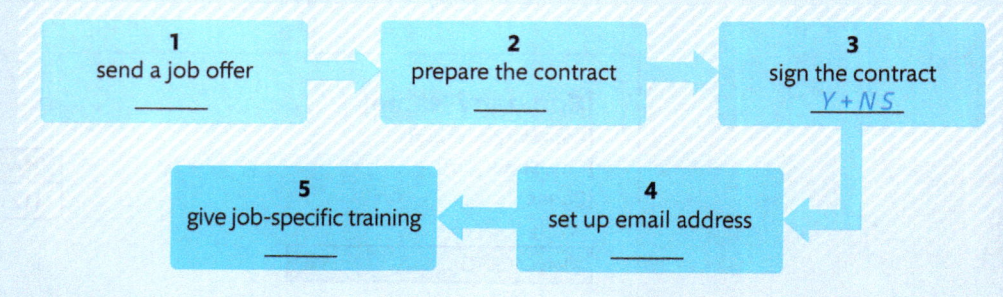

```
1                      2                         3
send a job offer  →   prepare the contract  →   sign the contract
                                                    Y + NS
                                                       ↓
5                      4
give job-specific  ←  set up email address
training
```

B Which stage(s) from the workflow in Exercise 3A does Paulo want to change?

C ▶ 7.4.2 Watch Part 2 of the video. Which stages in the process are <u>not</u> necessary with the new system?

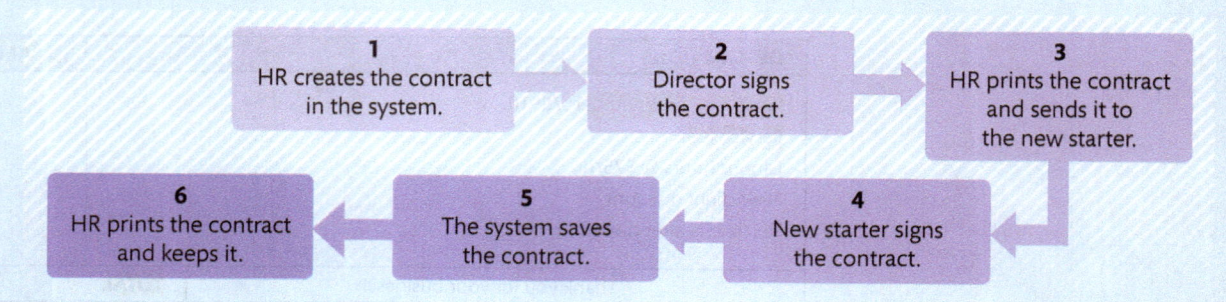

```
1                         2                      3
HR creates the contract → Director signs    →   HR prints the contract
in the system.            the contract.         and sends it to
                                                the new starter.
                                                       ↓
6                         5                      4
HR prints the contract ← The system saves   ←   New starter signs
and keeps it.            the contract.          the contract.
```

7.4 Work skills: Changing a workflow

4 Put the words in bold in the correct order.
1. **we don't why** use technology? _____
2. That's an interesting idea. **more tell me**. _____
3. **we can how** improve this? _____
4. **solution what's the**? _____
5. **use not why** an electronic contracts system? _____
6. **about not I'm sure** that. _____
7. Really? **that great sounds**. _____
8. **get could you** more information about this? _____
9. **think I should we** invite Mark from IT. _____
10. **a idea that's good**. _____

Speaking

> **MAKING AND RESPONDING TO SUGGESTIONS**
>
> **Giving ideas**
> I think we need to improve the process.
> Why don't we use technology?
> Why not use an electronic contracts system?
> I think we should invite Susie from HR.
>
> **Responding to ideas**
> What's the solution?
> How can we improve this?
> Could you get me more information about this?
> Really? That sounds great.
> That's interesting. Tell me more.
> That's a good idea.
> I'm not sure about that.
> OK, but I'm not totally convinced.

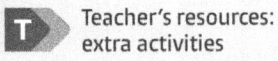

Teacher's resources: extra activities

5A Work in pairs. Imagine you are Yumiko and Paulo and are discussing the process for hiring new staff. Look at the list of tasks below and answer the questions.
- Do you need to add any stages?
- Are any stages <u>not</u> necessary?
- How long do you need for the complete process? A week? Two weeks? A month?

> - attend health and safety training
> - attend induction meetings
> - attend job-specific training
> - check qualifications and diplomas
> - check references
> - complete employee's details (address, bank details, emergency contact number, etc.)
> - discuss tasks
> - give medical certificate
> - give office tour
> - give qualifications and diplomas
> - give references
> - organise health and safety training
> - organise induction meetings
> - organise job-specific training
> - set up company account/email for new starter
> - sign the contract

B Use the stages from Exercise 5A to write a workflow. Decide <u>when</u> each stage should happen and <u>who</u> is responsible for each stage: *Human Resources* (HR), *New starter* (NS), *IT* or *Line Manager* (LM).
Before the first day:
- *sign the contract (HR + NS)*

C Describe and compare your workflow with another pair.

Self-assessment | I can discuss workflows and ways of improving a workflow.

BUSINESS WORKSHOP

How can we improve it?

Lesson outcome: Learners can discuss problems with a workflow and suggest improvements.

Identifying problems

1A Read the workflow. Tick (✓) what it is about.

- arranging a meeting with a client
- ordering a new part
- signing a contract

1. The Production Manager phones the supply office and tells them the product number and the number of items he/she needs.

2. The supply office emails the supplier who checks his/her inventory, the price and the delivery time.

3. The supply office phones the Production Manager, tells him/her the information and asks him/her to contact finance.

4. The Production Manager completes a form requesting the money and sends it to finance at head office by post.

5. When finance receive the form, they phone the Production Manager to check the information and approve the payment.

6. The Production Manager phones the supply office to notify them that finance approved the payment.

7. The supply office order the part.

8. The supplier sends the part to production.

B Look at the sentences (a–e). Which of these is <u>not</u> a possible problem with the workflow in Exercise 1A?

a The supply office write down the wrong product number.
b The Production Manager has to talk to different suppliers and doesn't have time.
c Important documents are lost in the post.
d Finance have to phone the Production Manager again and again to check the information because he/she is not in the office.
e The delivery is delayed because the supplier doesn't have the item(s) and has to order it/them from the manufacturer.

Talking about solutions

2 Work in groups of three. Have a meeting to improve the workflow in Exercise 1A.

Student A: Read the information below.
Student B: Look at page 118 and read the information.
Student C: Look at page 120 and read the information.

Student A

You are the Production Manager.

Ask the Supply Office Manager (Student B) and the Finance Manager (Student C) how the company can improve the situation.

Listen to their ideas and respond.

How can we improve this?
What's the solution?
That's interesting. Tell me more.
That sounds great.
Could you give me more information about that?

The new workflow

3A Choose the correct options in the new workflow.

1. *Notify / Complete* a form online to order the part.

2. *Tell / Request* the supply office and finance about the order.

3. *Approve / Download* the payment on the system.

4. *Remember / Inform* the supply office of the payment.

5. *Deliver / Order* the part online.

6. *Notify / Check* the Production Manager the part is ordered.

7. *Forget / Save* all the documents.

8. *Order / Send* the delivery date to the supply office and Production Manager.

B Work in pairs. Discuss who is responsible for each stage in the new workflow in Exercise 3A. The *Production Manager* (PM), the *Supply Office* (SO), *Finance* (F) or the *System* (S). Look at the role cards in Exercise 2 to help you.

Self-assessment: I can discuss problems with a workflow and suggest improvements.

Managing projects

8

Unit overview

8.1	**How long does it take?** **Lesson outcome:** Learners can talk about a supply chain and how long different stages take.	**Vocabulary:** Production **Communicative grammar:** Revision of the present **Video:** Making cars at the Morgan Motor Company **Task:** Explaining information on a database
8.2	**Reducing costs** **Lesson outcome:** Learners can talk about different ways of reducing company costs.	**Vocabulary:** Saving money **Reading:** An online interview **Communicative grammar:** Revision of the past **Writing:** Actions and results
8.3	**Planning projects** **Lesson outcome:** Learners can write about a plan for a project.	**Reading:** Scope statements **Communicative grammar:** Revision of the future **Writing:** Scope statements
8.4	**Work skills:** Giving feedback **Lesson outcome:** Learners can give feedback to a colleague.	**Video:** Feedback in the office **Speaking:** Giving feedback
8.5	**Business workshop:** Updates and feedback **Lesson outcome:** Learners can talk about, and give feedback on, the actions and results of a project.	**Reading:** A team update email **Writing:** Replying to an update **Speaking:** Giving feedback

Review 8: p.94   **Pronunciation:** 8.2 Pronouncing the letter 'o'   8.3 The vowel /ɜː/ p.103

8.1 How long does it take?

Lesson outcome Learners can talk about a supply chain and how long different stages take.

Lead-in **1** Label the parts of a supply chain.

> customer   factory   materials   shipping   shop   warehouse

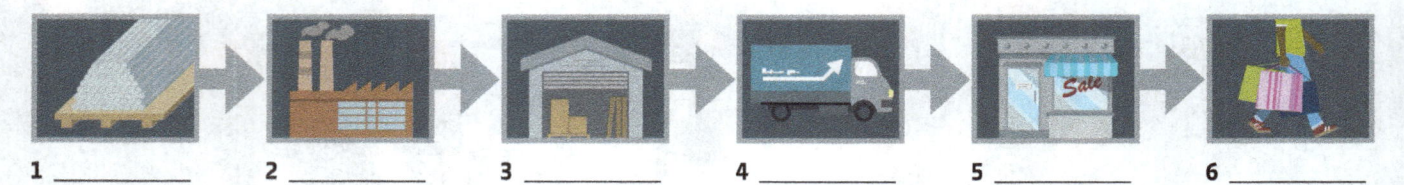

1 _____ 2 _____ 3 _____ 4 _____ 5 _____ 6 _____

Vocabulary   Production

2 Match 1–4 with a–d.

1 **Manufacturing** happens at our factory in Ghent, Belgium. They build 500 models a week.
2 **Demand** is high for our new phone. Lots of customers want to buy a Ti111 and we have to make more!
3 Product **inspection** is very important. If our products don't work, we lose customers.
4 The **lead time** depends on how many orders we get and how many items we have in the warehouse. Sometimes clients have to wait for three days, sometimes three weeks.

a How much customers want a product
b Checking the product
c Time from the order to the delivery of the product
d Making the product

3 Read the sentences and definitions. Which term in bold completes each sentence?

1 When a product is _____ , there are no items in the shop or warehouse.
   in stock (= The seller has the product available.)
   out of stock (= The seller does not have the product available.)
2 On a _____ , customers ask to change the colour or design of the product.
   standard model = (The product is the normal type.)
   custom model = (The product is different to the normal type.)

Teacher's resources: extra activities

4 Complete the text with the words in bold in Exercises 2 and 3.

WORKING AT CORTADINO CARS: FAQs FOR NEW EMPLOYEES

What can the customer buy?
There are two options:
- a(n) ¹_____ : ninety percent of our sales. The customer chooses from a range of popular options.
- a(n) ²_____ : ten percent of our sales. The customer wants something different (engine, colour, etc).

Do we have it?
- Cars that are ³_____ have a ✓ on the system.
- Cars that are ⁴_____ have a ✗ on the system.
If we don't have the model the customer wants, or the customer wants something different, please order from the factory.

What happens after ordering a car from the factory?
There are three main stages:
1 ⁵_____ , when our team in Asia build the cars.
2 Shipping, when our team in Asia send the cars around the world.
3 Final ⁶_____ when we receive the car.
Normally the ⁷_____ for a model we have available is five to fifteen working days, and for factory orders it is eight to twelve weeks. However, when there is high ⁸_____ for a popular model, this can take longer.

8.1 How long does it take?

Listening
A training session

5A 🔊 8.01 Listen to the first part of a training session at Cortadino Cars. Complete the database file.

el name:
adino ¹_____ ²
el type (standard/custom):
_____
ock? (✓/✗): ³___
ufacturing: ⁴___ working days
ping: ⁵___ weeks
ection: ⁶___ working days
d time: ⁷___ weeks

B 🔊 8.02 Listen to the second part of the training session. Are the sentences *true* (T) or *false* (F)?
1 The N20 is in stock.
2 There are fifty models in the Liège factory.
3 Cortadino Cars need five to six working days to ship the car from Liège.
4 Final inspection takes three to four working days.
5 The lead time is six to eight working days.

Communicative grammar

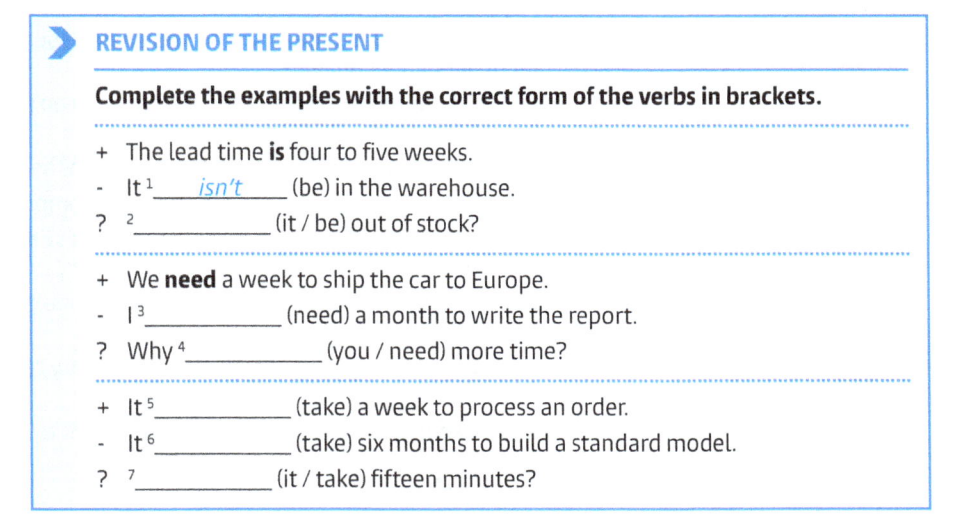

> **REVISION OF THE PRESENT**
>
> Complete the examples with the correct form of the verbs in brackets.
>
> + The lead time **is** four to five weeks.
> - It ¹ _isn't_ (be) in the warehouse.
> ? ² _____ (it / be) out of stock?
>
> + We **need** a week to ship the car to Europe.
> - I ³ _____ (need) a month to write the report.
> ? Why ⁴ _____ (you / need) more time?
>
> + It ⁵ _____ (take) a week to process an order.
> - It ⁶ _____ (take) six months to build a standard model.
> ? ⁷ _____ (it / take) fifteen minutes?

6 Complete the sentences with the correct form of the words in brackets.
1 We _____ (need) five working days to build a standard model.
2 That product _____ (be) in stock in our warehouse.
3 Normally, shipping _____ (not take) more than ten working days.
4 _____ (you / need) five working days to ship the product?
5 _____ (the lead time / be) longer than a month?
6 It _____ (take) a long time to find a new supplier.

Teacher's resources: extra activities

VIDEO
7A ▶ 8.1.1 Watch the video. Tick (✓) the topics the speaker mentions.

| car colour | demand | invoices | lead time | warehouse |

B Watch again. Are the sentences *true* (T) or *false* (F)? Correct the false sentences.
1 The Morgan Motor Company build fifteen cars every week.
2 The Morgan Motor Company manufacture all the parts at the factory.
3 Customers can choose from 50,000 paint colours.
4 It takes eight hours to paint the car.
5 The Morgan Motor Company ship seventy-five percent of their cars to other countries.
6 When demand is high, the lead time can change.

> **TASK**
>
> **8** Student A: Look at page 120. Student B: Look at page 121.

Self-assessment: I can talk about a supply chain and how long different stages take.

8.2 Reducing costs

Lesson outcome — Learners can talk about different ways of reducing company costs.

Lead-in 1 What percentage of your budget do you spend on these things?

> clothes   food   free-time activities   rent/mortgage   transport

Vocabulary Saving money

2 Look at the phrases in bold. What do they mean? Underline the key words that explain the phrases.

1 We often **review expenses**. It's important to <u>see how we spend money</u>. Last year, we spent forty percent of our budget on rent!
2 My company likes to **automate tasks**. Using a machine to do some of our work is great! Now we have more time for other things.
3 Employees can **work remotely**. Last week I didn't work in the office – I worked at home.
4 We need to **upgrade** our **technology**. Can we buy new computers and software, please?
5 We **outsource work** to a company in France. They help us with our work – they did our accounts last year.
6 Can we **negotiate with** the suppliers? I want to talk about a change to the contract – we need a better price.
7 Could we **relocate to** that new business park out of the city centre? My old company moved offices and they saved a lot of money.
8 How can we **save energy**? Turn off the computers at night to use less electricity.

3 Match 1–8 with a–h.

1 Yesterday I negotiated
2 We outsourced our
3 We saved
4 Last month we relocated
5 Last week I worked
6 We upgraded
7 We reviewed our
8 The company automated

a energy by moving to a more modern and efficient office.
b to Berlin. Our new office is great!
c with their sales team. They gave us a better price.
d work to an accountant. We had no time.
e that task, so employees don't have to do it.
f expenses yesterday. We have a big plan to save money.
g the company's technology. Now, we all have tablets!
h remotely – I was in Poland!

Teacher's resources: extra activities

Reading An online interview

4A Read the interview. Which sentence is <u>false</u>?

1 Mr Kowalczyk checked company costs.
2 The company had problems with an accountant.
3 The employees didn't like the new software.

Q: You reduced your costs by twenty-five percent! How did you do it?

A: Firstly, I reviewed the company's expenses to see how to save money. Our rent was very expensive! So we relocated to a different building in the same city. But, the old office was bigger, so employees now work remotely two days a week. It saves money *and* employees are happy to work at home! In the new office, we also changed things: we bought LED lights and saved energy.

Q: Was it difficult to make changes?

A: Yes, it was. For example, we outsourced work to an accountant, but he didn't complete the tasks – he didn't have time. So we negotiated a new contract with him for extra hours but he said no!

Q: Did the employees like the changes?

A: Yes, they loved the changes! For example, we upgraded our technology. The new software, on the same computers, automated tasks that were very boring. Employees now have more time for other work.

Mr Kowalczyk

B Read the interview again. What did the company do?

> buy new computers   move office   save money   save time for employees   sell more products

8.2 Reducing costs

Communicative grammar

> **REVISION OF THE PAST**
>
> Complete the examples with the correct form of the verbs in brackets. Some verbs are irregular.
>
> + Our rent **was** very expensive.
> - It ¹_____ (be) a good idea.
> ? Why ²_____ (it / be) a problem?
>
> + We **relocated** to a different building in the same city.
> - He ³_____ (complete) his tasks.
> ? How ⁴_____ (you / save) energy?
>
> ? ⁵_____ (you / sell) more this year or last year?

Teacher's resources: extra activities

5 Look at the comments section of the interview in Exercise 4A. Complete the comments with the correct form of the verbs in brackets. Some verbs are irregular.

Elvira — Managing Director of Microdo Tech

'Last year we ¹_____ (reduce) the number of tasks employees have because we ²_____ (automate) our customer service system. The employees ³_____ (be) very happy.

We also ⁴_____ (negotiate) with our software supplier. We ⁵_____ (buy) a new software package for the sales department at a good price. But the training took a long time and the employees ⁶_____ (not complete) it. So in the end, we ⁷_____ (not save) money in sales.'

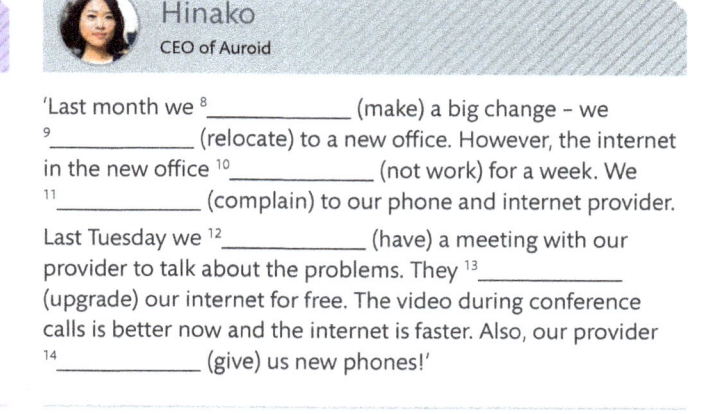

Hinako — CEO of Auroid

'Last month we ⁸_____ (make) a big change – we ⁹_____ (relocate) to a new office. However, the internet in the new office ¹⁰_____ (not work) for a week. We ¹¹_____ (complain) to our phone and internet provider. Last Tuesday we ¹²_____ (have) a meeting with our provider to talk about the problems. They ¹³_____ (upgrade) our internet for free. The video during conference calls is better now and the internet is faster. Also, our provider ¹⁴_____ (give) us new phones!'

→ **page 103** See Pronunciation bank: Pronouncing the letter 'o'

Writing

6A Look at the table. Which pairs of actions and results do Elvira and Hinako write about in Exercise 5? Write 'E' or 'H' next to the correct line. Only four pairs are used.

+

Action	Result	
upgrade our technology	→ have better conference calls with clients	
review company expenses	→ have a better budget and can save money	
automate services	→ have happy employees	E
save energy	→ reduce costs by five percent	

−

Action	Result	
relocate to a new office	→ have internet problems	
negotiate with our software supplier	→ have a bad training experience	
outsource work	→ receive poor-quality work	
work remotely	→ employees talk only by email	

B You are the CEO at Catantere, a digital design company. Write an online comment like the ones in Exercise 5.
- Explain how you reduced costs.
- Use one positive (+) and one negative (−) pair of actions and results from the tables in Exercise 6A.
- Use different ideas to Elvira and Hinako.

Self-assessment — I can talk about different ways of reducing company costs.

8.3 Planning projects

Lesson outcome   Learners can write about a plan for a project.

Lead-in

1A Match the people with the pictures.

> architects   chefs   fashion designers   teachers

B Match the people in Exercise 1A with the tasks in the box.

> design student tests   design summer/winter collections   order food supplies
> plan building size   plan lessons   plan menus   plan fashion shows   prepare floor plans

C What tasks do you do in your job?

I'm a Product Manager. I plan the sales and marketing campaigns for our products.

Reading   Scope statements

2A Read the two scope statements. Choose the correct title for each. There are two extra titles.

> Changes in IT   Project management   Reducing costs   Three-month plan

scope statement: a written plan that explains what a project will do, and how

a _____

This project will upgrade our technology at Lever&Smith Design. It will take three months to complete. Firstly, we will improve the internet connection and buy new routers for the office. The new internet service will be faster than our old system. Then we will move all employees from Mak25 to Chimen Pro software. This won't happen before the conference in September, but it will happen before October. The result is that all employees will be able to work online more efficiently.

b _____

This project will review Lever&Smith Design's expenses. We will hire Impleoni Accounting to do this. The project will start in three months. Firstly, Impleoni Accounting will look at all the company's expenses in the last two years. Then they will have meetings with managers to discuss the expenses. Finally, they will provide a plan to reduce Lever&Smith Design's expenses. The deadline is the 31st December, so this means that we won't make any company changes this year.

B Read the two scope statements again. Which scope statement does this information refer to?

		Scope statement a	Scope statement b
1	The project will make technology better at the company.	✓	
2	The project will use company information from previous years.		
3	The project will outsource work to a different company.		
4	The project will finish in three months.		
5	The project will need some managers to attend meetings.		

→ page 103   See Pronunciation bank: The vowel /ɜː/

8.3 Planning projects

Communicative grammar

> **REVISION OF THE FUTURE**
>
> Complete the examples with the correct form of the verbs in brackets. Use contractions if possible.
>
> + This project ¹_____ (review) Lever&Smith Design's expenses.
> + We ²_____ (improve) the internet connection.
>
> − This ³_____ (happen) before the conference in September.
> − The project ⁴_____ (continue) next year.
>
> ? **Will** we **be able to** see the report from Impleoni Accounting?
> ? When ⁵_____ (the changes / happen)?

3 Match 1–6 with a–f.

1 We won't buy new
2 We will hire more
3 The company won't
4 I will complete my
5 I will travel
6 My colleagues won't attend the

a move offices in the next three years.
b conference next month.
c employees next year.
d for work next month.
e project this month.
f computers this year.

4 Complete the email update with the correct form of the words in brackets.

Project update, 3rd September

Dear all,

I would like to give you more information about the next step of our project to upgrade Lever&Smith Design's technology.

As you know, our new software will be here soon, and I can now answer your questions:

- ¹_____ I _____ (be) able to continue using the Mak25 database?
  No, you ²_____ . The Mak25 database ³_____ (not work) after October 1st.

- ⁴_____ all employees _____ (receive) training on the new software at the same time?
  Yes, they ⁵_____ . All employees ⁶_____ (have) their training on Monday 20th – ten days before the move to Chimen Pro.

- ⁷_____ we _____ (lose) the data from the Mak25 database?
  No, you ⁸_____ . The IT team ⁹_____ (transfer) all the data from Mak25 to the new Chimen Pro database next week.

I'm sure the new software ¹⁰_____ (be) a great success!

Kind regards,

Teacher's resources: extra activities

Writing

5 Look at the two scope statements in Exercise 2A again. Number the words/phrases in the box in the order they are used.

> Finally,   Firstly,   The result is that / This means that   Then   This project will *1*

6 You are the Project Manager at Tookull Computers. Write a scope statement for the project your company will do next year. Use the notes on page 116 and the phrases in Exercise 5 to help you.

Self-assessment   I can write about a plan for a project.

8.4 WORK SKILLS
Giving feedback

Lesson outcome — Learners can give feedback to a colleague.

Lead-in 1A Match the photos (A–F) with the sentences (1–6).

1 A really nice team-building activity, good work!
2 Nice work – the new model looks great!
3 A fantastic conference this year!
4 The new offices are perfect – well done!
5 Sales are up! Good job!
6 The slides are very good, thanks!

B How often do you give or receive feedback?

VIDEO 2A ▶ 8.4.1 Watch Parts 1 and 2 of the video. What is each part about? Tick (✓) one topic from each box.

Part 1
| reducing costs   reducing lead time |
| shipping |

Part 2
| a presentation   a new product |
| customer service |

B Watch both parts of the video again. Match 1–2 with a–e and 3–4 with f–j. There is one extra option in each section.

Part 1: Rachel
1 Positives
2 Areas to improve

a ask for help if you need it
b communicate every day with the team
c finding new warehouses
d save more money
e negotiating dates with suppliers

Part 2: Andrea
3 Positives
4 Areas to improve

f answering questions
g show the clients our customer reviews
h making the presentation slides
i selling the product to clients
j invite more people

84

8.4 Work skills: Giving feedback

3 Match 1–5 with a–e and 6–10 with f–j.

1 Do you
2 I just want to say – great
3 We're very
4 Great job
5 Well done on negotiating the dates with

a work on Thursday!
b the suppliers.
c selling the product to our clients.
d happy with the project.
e have a moment?

6 This means that we can
7 The result is that
8 Try to communicate every
9 In future, invite
10 Next time, remember

f to ask for help if you need it!
g the clients are now very interested.
h more people!
i day with the team.
j reduce the lead time by two days.

Speaking

> **GIVING FEEDBACK**

Being positive
Well done!
Fantastic work!
We're very happy with your work.

Talking about positive areas
Great job managing the project.
Well done on negotiating with the vendors.
Good work writing the report.

Talking about results
This means that we can increase sales by five percent.
The result is that we can automate tasks.

Suggesting areas to improve
Try to review expenses every month.
Remember to have a progress meeting with the team.
In future, ask for a higher price.

Responding to feedback
Sure.
Of course.
Thanks!

Teacher's resources: extra activities

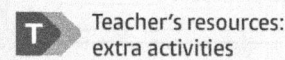

4 Choose the correct word.

Do you ¹*have / need* a moment? I just want to say we're very happy ²*with / on* your work – great job arranging the conference! Well done ³*on / about* finding the conference room and ⁴*well / good* work inviting those colleagues to give presentations. The ⁵*result / means* is that the employees now understand more about our plan for next year. In future, invite marketing, and ⁶*have to / try to* provide more food!

5 Work with a partner.
Student A: Follow the instructions below.
Student B: Look at page 120.

Student A
You work for Herranz&Janssen, a manufacturing company. Read the notes and think about what you can say. Then give feedback to your employee (Student B).

Project:	Reviewing expenses
Positives:	Check the expenses every week
	Write the reports
Result:	Reduce costs by two percent
To improve:	Meet the deadline
	Have progress meetings with production

Self-assessment I can give feedback to a colleague.

BUSINESS WORKSHOP

Updates and feedback

Lesson outcome: Learners can talk about, and give feedback on, the actions and results of a project.

A team update

1 Read the email. Are the sentences *true* (T) or *false* (F)?

Subject: Team update – X290

Hi Alex and Sam,

An update on the X290 phone:

- We now have the date and location of the next progress meeting with management. It will be on 31st May at the Rotterdam office. Ranjit will send an email about hotels and travel to Rotterdam.
- It will take marketing two weeks to finish the webpage for the X290. This means we won't be able to review it until April. Ellen will tell us when it's ready.
- Unfortunately, I can't come to the supplier meeting on Friday because I have a conference call. Alex, can you send me the minutes, please?

Also Alex, what's the situation with the supply chain for Central Europe? Did you talk to the suppliers? And did you find a new warehouse?

And Sam, where are we with the product design? Did you upgrade the phone to the new processor? And did you change the product material?

Please let me know because I need to write the product report for the Rotterdam meeting.

Regards,
Tom
Global Product Director

---

1. The X290 team have a meeting with their bosses to discuss the product in May.
2. The team will be able to review the webpage in March.
3. Tom wants Sam to send him the minutes of the supplier meeting.
4. Tom asks Alex about the supply chain and Sam about the product launch.
5. Tom will use Alex and Sam's answers to prepare for the meeting with their bosses on 31st May.

2A Read Alex's reply to Tom and complete the table.

Subject: Team update – X290

Hi Tom,

You asked me about the supply chain. Here is my update.

- We negotiated with the suppliers in Poland last week and the result is that we can reduce the manufacturing costs of the X290 by 4.5 percent.
- We also found a new warehouse in Munich last Friday. This means that we can reduce the lead time for Central Europe by twenty-four hours because the shipping time is now faster.

Regards,
Alex

Action	Result
Negotiate with ¹ _the suppliers in Poland_ (last week)	² _____
³ _____	Reduce lead time for Central Europe by twenty-four hours because ⁴ _____

B Imagine you are Sam. Write a reply to Tom like the one in Exercise 2A. Reply to the questions below from Tom's email. Use the information in the table to help you.

> And Sam, where are we with the product design? Did you upgrade the phone to the new processor? And did you change the product material?

Action	Result
Upgrade the processor and software on the X290 (last month)	There is high demand for the new technology and software from our customers.
Change the product materials (last week)	The product is now higher quality and we can sell it at a higher price.

Giving feedback

3 Work in pairs. Take turns to imagine you are Tom. Give feedback to your employee.

Student A: Look at page 121 and give feedback to Alex.
Student B: Look at page 120 and give feedback to Sam.

Self-assessment: I can talk about, and give feedback on, the actions and results of a project.

1 REVIEW

Vocabulary

1 Complete the sentences with the words in brackets.
1 Is Rafa from ___Spain___, or is he ___Mexican___? (Mexican / Spain)
2 Maria isn't from _____. She's _____. (Argentina / Brazilian)
3 I'm _____. I'm from _____. (China / Chinese)
4 Is Dugie _____, or is he from _____? (British / Ireland)
5 We're from _____. We're _____. (India / Indian)
6 Kenji isn't from _____, he's _____. (Japanese / Poland)

2 Complete the form with the words in the box.

> address   cell   given   last   middle
> nationality   number   postcode   title

1 _____	Mrs
first/2 _____ name	Sarah
3 _____ name	Jane
surname/4 _____ name	Smith
5 _____	American
home 6 _____	22 West Street, Denver, Colorado
7 _____/zip code	80744
passport/ID card 8 _____	445990011
mobile/9 _____/phone number	1-559-189-0190

3 Complete the words.
1 d_a_r_k_ ≠ l_i_g_h_t_
2 s_____ ≠ l_____
3 n_____ ≠ q_____
4 m_____ ≠ o___-f_____

Grammar

4 Complete the dialogues with the correct form of *be*. Use contractions if possible.
A: They ¹___aren't___ from India.
B: No? Where ²_____ they from?
C: ³_____ you from Spain?
D: No, I ⁴_____. I ⁵_____ from Germany.
E: ⁶_____ she Mexican?
F: No, she ⁷_____. She ⁸_____ from Spain.
G: My name ⁹_____ Alexandra, and this ¹⁰_____ David.
H: Where ¹¹_____ you from?
G: We ¹²_____ from Brazil.
I: ¹³_____ they from Japan?
J: No, they ¹⁴_____. They¹⁵_____ from Mexico.

5 Match 1-3 with a-c and 4-6 with d-f.
1 There's   a gym in the Frankfurt office.
2 There are   b a warehouse in Katowice.
3 There's no   c two offices in Spain.

4 There are no   d a restaurant near the office.
5 There's   e managers in the office.
6 There's no   f canteen.

Functional language

6 Choose the correct option.
1 Good morning. How may I help you?
   a I'm here to see Miss Pohl.
   b I'm sorry, she's not at her desk.
   c My name's Rudy Fowler.
2 Could you repeat that, please?
   a Sure. E-V-A …
   b Yes, it's Eva Conway.
   c Could you spell that, please?
3 Have a seat, please.
   a Good to see you, too!
   b Thank you.
   c Yes, please.
4 Would you like some tea or coffee?
   a Tea, please. Thanks.
   b Sugar, please. No milk.
   c Would you like milk or sugar?
5 Please come in.
   a After you.
   b Yes, please.
   c How about some water?

2 REVIEW

Vocabulary

1 Choose a verb and put it in the correct form to complete the sentences.

1 I _manage_ the customer services team. (make/manage/sell)
2 Patricia _____ for a pharmaceutical company. (answer/check/work)
3 The company _____ sports equipment online. (manage/sell/solve)
4 Paul _____ meetings with staff and clients. (check/have/make)
5 The IT Specialist _____ our technical problems. (answer/provide/solve)
6 Dania _____ in the IT department as a software designer. (have/sell/work)
7 The company _____ air transport services. (make/provide/solve)
8 We _____ websites for e-commerce companies. (design/work/write)

2 🔊 R 2.01 Write the missing numbers and words. Then listen and repeat.

170	1_____
2_____	five hundred and twenty-five
815	3_____
4_____	two thousand and thirty-six
44,208	5_____
6_____	sixty-three thousand, nine hundred and eighteen
100,000	7_____
8_____	three hundred and twenty-one thousand
752,400	9_____
10_____	a million / one million

Grammar

3 Complete the replies with the negative form. Use contractions if possible.

1 **A:** He works at the weekend.
   B: No, he _doesn't work_ at the weekend. He works Monday to Friday.
2 **A:** They design shoes.
   B: No, they _____ shoes. They design clothes.
3 **A:** The company has over 200 warehouse robots.
   B: No, it _____ over 200, it has over 1,000.
4 **A:** She studies in the afternoon.
   B: No, she _____ in the afternoon. She studies in the morning.
5 **A:** You spend a week in the head office every month.
   B: No, I _____ a week in the head office. I spend two or three days there.

4A Put the words in the correct order to make questions.

1 do / work / Where / you / ?
_____
2 do / do / you / What / ?
_____
3 work / you / at / What / do / do / ?
_____
4 job / Do / your / like / you / ?
_____
5 you / What / work / do / days / ?
_____
6 work / Do / for / travel / you / ?
_____
7 your / do / What / you / time / in / free / do / ?
_____

B Match the questions (1–7) in Exercise 4A with the answers (a–g).

a I'm an Engineer and Project Manager. ____
b Yes, I go to Bratislava every month. ____
c I work for a car manufacturer. We're based in Ingolstadt. ____
d I spend time with my family and friends. ____
e I manage my department and have meetings with the project team. ____
f Yes, I do. It's very interesting. ____
g I work Monday to Friday. ____

C Write answers to the questions in Exercise 4A about yourself.

Functional language

5 Choose the correct word to complete the sentences.

Fran: Hello! My name's Fran.
Kyra: Hi! I'm Kyra. Nice ¹*talking to / to meet* you.
Fran: Which department ²*are you in / do you do*?
Kyra: I'm in purchasing. And ³*what about / what are* you?
Fran: I'm new here. I'm ⁴*at / in* the HR department.
Kyra: I see. What ⁵*do you / is your* do?
Fran: I'm ⁶*a / an* intern.
Kyra: And what ⁷*do / does* an intern do in HR?
Fran: I answer the phones and take notes at meetings. ⁸*Do you / And you*?
Kyra: I'm ⁹*a / an* Purchasing Assistant. I phone suppliers and make orders.
Fran: ¹⁰*That's / That* sounds good. ¹¹*Do / Does* you know Linda?
Kyra: Yes, she's my manager.
Fran: Really? She's my sister.
Kyra: ¹²*That's / That* interesting. Well, nice talking to you, Fran.
Fran: And you, Kyra. ¹³*See you / Meet you* later.

3 REVIEW

Vocabulary

1 Match the months with the seasons for your country.

| April   August   December   February |
| January   July   June   March   May |
| November   October   September |

Winter: _____
Spring: _____
Summer: _____
Autumn: _____

2 🔊 R 3.01 Listen and write the dates you hear.
1 _____23rd November 2015_____
2 _____
3 _____
4 _____
5 _____
6 _____
7 _____
8 _____

3 🔊 R 3.02 Listen and number the times in the order you hear them.

a ___   08.45
b ___   14.00
c ___   19.45
d ___   11.30
e ___   18.30
f ___   17.30

Grammar

4 Complete the sentences and questions with *can* or *can't*.
1 I come to the meeting (+)
   _____I can come to the meeting._____
2 you come to the meeting (?)
   _____
3 They come to the meeting (-)
   _____
4 He finish the report (-)
   _____
5 she finish the report (?)
   _____
6 We finish the report (+)
   _____
7 They meet on Wednesday (+)
   _____
8 I meet on Wednesday (-)
   _____
9 we meet on Wednesday (?)
   _____

5 Complete the sentences with *was* or *were*.
1 There _____ a problem with the report.
2 _____ you in the meeting yesterday?
3 I _____ late to meet the client.
4 We _____ (-) at the conference.
5 They _____ with a client yesterday.
6 _____ he in the office yesterday?
7 She _____ (-) at work last Wednesday.
8 Where _____ the hotel?

Functional language

6 Complete the sentences with the phrases in the box.

| aren't finished   can we meet   I think we |
| I think we can   is everything   what can we |
| what's the situation   where are |

1 _____ we with the report?
2 We _____ . I'm sorry.
3 OK, _____ do to solve this?
4 And _____ with sales?
5 _____ the deadline?
6 No. _____ need more time.
7 _____ on schedule?
8 Yes, _____ finish it by Wednesday.

4 REVIEW

Vocabulary

1 Complete the sentences with the past form of the words in the box.

give   go   have   make   say   see   send   write

1 I _____ sorry for my mistake.
2 He _____ twelve phone calls yesterday.
3 I _____ to meet a client on Monday.
4 They _____ fifty emails last week.
5 We _____ the invoice last month.
6 She _____ four meetings yesterday.
7 I _____ my manager this morning.
8 We _____ our customers a discount last year.

2 Complete the sentences with the words in the box.

about   ask   check   contact   for   send   that   to

1 _____ your spam folder.
2 Check _____ it's connected to your computer.
3 Let's _____ the client a message.
4 _____ the customer by email.
5 You can _____ IT to help.
6 Ask your manager _____ a new ID card.
7 Send the document _____ the printer.
8 Contact the supplier _____ the invoice.

Grammar

3 Complete the sentences with the past form of the words in brackets. Some verbs are irregular.

1 We _____ (work) late last week.
2 I _____ (send) you an email yesterday.
3 The client _____ (say) thank you for the report.
4 We _____ (stop) selling that model last year.
5 We _____ (plan) the project last week.
6 You _____ (write) the report yesterday.
7 I _____ (start) my new job yesterday.
8 She _____ (have) a meeting last Monday.
9 They both _____ (study) at Cambridge University.

4 Write questions and answers using the prompts.

1 **A:** you / work late / last night / ?
   _____
   B: No. I / not work / late last night / .
   _____

2 **A:** they / finish / the report yesterday / ?
   _____
   B: No. They / not finish / the report yesterday / .
   _____

3 **A:** he / meet / a new client on Tuesday / ?
   _____
   B: No. He / not meet / a new client on Tuesday / .
   _____

4 **A:** we / give / the presentation last Friday / ?
   _____
   B: No. We / not give / the presentation last Friday / .
   _____

Functional language

5 Complete the sentences with the phrases in the box.

| call you when   can I help   could choose |
| give you your   order a new   what's the |
you change   you try turning

1 How _____ you?
2 Did _____ the battery?
3 I can _____ money back.
4 I'll _____ one.
5 _____ problem?
6 Did _____ it off?
7 You _____ a different one.
8 I'll _____ it's ready.

5 REVIEW

Vocabulary

1 Choose the correct word to complete the sentences.
1 How often do you *have / make* meetings?
2 I *have / visit* suppliers every day.
3 Do you *visit / make* phone calls every day?
4 We *make / visit* clients once a week.
5 Do you *write / make* minutes in your job?
6 I *make / write* 100 emails a day.

2 Complete the sentences with *product* or *meeting*.
1 Can we arrange a _____ for next week?
2 Our supplier has a large _____ range.
3 I received the _____ specifications yesterday.
4 I need to postpone the _____ until next week.
5 The _____ quality is very good.
6 We can have the _____ tomorrow.
7 The _____ launch is next month.
8 We need to cancel the _____ . The client can't come.

Grammar

3 Complete the sentences with the correct form of the words in brackets.
1 We a meeting at the moment (not have)
   We aren't having a meeting at the moment.
2 I to the client now (not talk)
   _____
3 They the product launch right now (not prepare)
   _____
4 I a new car at the moment (buy)
   _____
5 We the presentation slides now (make)
   _____
6 She a report at the moment (write)
   _____
7 He for work right now (not travel)
   _____
8 You a supplier at the moment (visit)
   _____

4 Write sentences and questions about future plans using the prompts.
1 I / meet / a new client / next week / .
   _____
2 She / give / a presentation / in two weeks / .
   _____
3 We / not go / on a business trip / tomorrow / .
   _____
4 he / send / the report / tomorrow / ?
   _____
5 You / not go / the product launch / next month / .
   _____
6 We / visit / our supplier / next week / .
   _____
7 I / work late / tomorrow / .
   _____
8 they / have / a meeting / next Thursday / ?
   _____

Functional language

5 Match 1–8 with a–h.
1 Could I ask you for   a 's no problem.
2 That   b ask Julia.
3 I'm really sorry   c help you?
4 You could   d some help?
5 Can I   e but I'm too busy.
6 No, I   f 'm fine. Thanks.
7 Could I ask a   g favour?
8 That would   h be great.

6 REVIEW

Vocabulary

1 Complete the missing words.
1. It's d_____ to park in the city centre. There are no spaces!
2. The city is very b_____ for me. It's big and noisy. I prefer the countryside.
3. We have a very s_____ office now – the old one was very small.
4. We work in a nice, old building that's very t_____ .
5. My office is a s_____ walk from the train station – only three minutes.
6. I'm c_____ to my office. It's a ten-minute walk from home.
7. My train journey to work is very, very l_____ . It's more than an hour.
8. I have an e_____ journey to work, just one bus.

2 Complete the table with the words and numbers in the box.

$2,400 $60   30 days from order   40
60 days from date of invoice   Zindex A320 Toner

QUOTE FOR TONER	
Product name:	
Unit price:	
Number of units:	
Delivery time:	
Payment terms:	
Total price:	

Grammar

3 Complete the email with the correct form of the words in brackets.

Hi team,

I'd like to inform you that we're moving offices next month. Our new office will be ¹_____ (modern) and ²_____ (light) than our office at the moment. It's a ³_____ (short) walk to a bus stop than our walk now, too. The space is ⁴_____ (big) and the rent is ⁵_____ (cheap) than our current office. Unfortunately, it's in a ⁶_____ (noisy) part of town than our old office. Also, if you travel by train, you will have a ⁷_____ (expensive) journey than at the moment. However, I think the new office will be ⁸_____ (good) than where we are now!

4 Put the bold words in the correct order.
1. If **fifty** / **units** / **we order** / , / **will** / **get** / **we** a discount.
   If we order fifty units, we will get a discount.
2. **choose** / **we** / **if** the standard package, **it** / **cost** / **will** $500.
   _____
3. **you** / **if** / **offer** us a discount, **buy** / **we** / **will** a hundred.
   _____
4. If **order** / **today** / **you** / , / we **deliver** / **will** / **tomorrow**.
   _____
5. **you** / **if** / **have** a problem, I **help** / **will** / **you**.
   _____
6. If **asks** / **he** / **the** / **clients** / , / **tell** / **will** / **they** him.
   _____
7. If **the** / **screen** / **you** / **look** / **at** / , / **see** / **will** / **you** a diagram.
   _____
8. **move** / **we** / **if** offices, we **will** / **more** / **space** / **have**.
   _____

Functional language

5 Complete the sentences with the phrases in the box.

as you   can see   if you   look at   on the slide
slide shows   you can   you look   you'll see

1. Let's _____ customer satisfaction.
2. This _____ three line graphs.
3. _____ can see _____ , sales were higher in Q1 than in Q2.
4. As you _____ from the bar chart, we spend more on deliveries.
5. _____ look at the table, _____ see that the sales are lower by fifteen percent.
6. If _____ at the third row, _____ our costs.

7 REVIEW

Vocabulary

1 Complete the sentences with the words in the box.

| approve   enter   issues   notify   supply   request |

1 Finance has to _____ the payment before I can buy the product.
2 Kane's Ltd _____ our ink and paper, we have a contract with them.
3 To create a new purchase order, _____ the supplier's details into the system.
4 I need to _____ a new machine from production. Can you approve it?
5 I'll _____ the supplier that we will make the payment today.
6 The system _____ the invoice automatically and sends it to the customer.

2 Replace the words in bold with the words in the box with a similar meaning.

| clear   complicated   excellent   is efficient
  is reliable   is unreliable   poor   simple |

1 They have **very, very good** customer service.
2 The ordering process is **very easy**.
3 The product was **not good** quality.
4 The website was **easy to understand**.
5 The delivery company **always delivers on time**.
6 The manual is **really difficult to understand**.
7 The team **finish their work quickly**.
8 The delivery company **never delivers on time**.

Grammar

3 Choose the correct form of *have to* to complete the sentences.

1 We *has to / have to / don't have* send the report by 8 o'clock tonight.
2 He *has to / have to / don't have to* start at 9 o'clock on Monday.
3 *Do you have to / Does you have to* work late tonight?
4 You *has to / have to / don't have to* meet me at reception but you can if you want to.
5 *Do she have to / Does she have to* meet the supplier?
6 She *has to / have to / don't have to / doesn't have to* go to the client's office next week but it's OK if she does.
7 **A:** Do you have to go to work tomorrow?
  B: *No, I don't have / No, I don't.*
8 I *has to / have to / don't have to* leave at 6 p.m. or I'll be late.

4 Put the phrases in the correct order to make instructions.

1 by Monday / the report / complete
  _____
2 an email / send / to finance
  _____
3 contact / by phone / the supplier
  _____
4 the document / remember / to save
  _____
5 to email / the customer / don't forget
  _____
6 change / in the photocopier / the paper
  _____
7 click / on the system / 'create invoice'
  _____
8 the payment / in the system / approve
  _____

Functional language

5 Choose the correct words to complete the dialogue.

A: How can we [1]*improve / manage* the invoice system?
B: Why [2]*not / don't* we use a computer system?
A: Really? That [3]*sounds / listens* good.
B: Yes, I [4]*want / think* we should create invoices in a new system.
A: That's interesting. Tell me [5]*more / less*.
B: I think we [6]*have to / need* a system that issues invoices automatically.
A: Could you get me some more [7]*information / plan*?
B: OK, why [8]*don't / not* have a meeting with IT to talk about it?

8 REVIEW

Vocabulary

1 Match 1–6 with a–f.
1 There is high
2 Final inspection is the
3 We have more than 2,000
4 The lead time is two weeks:
5 The standard model
6 Manufacturing is the longest part of the

a items in stock at our shop in Clermont-Ferrand.
b is blue, with a Ko31 processor.
c demand for our services at the moment – we need more employees!
d one week for production and one week for shipping.
e process because we have old machines in our factory.
f last thing we do before shipping to the customer.

2 Complete the sentences with the words in the box. There are two extra words.

> automate   negotiate   outsource   relocate
> review   save   upgrade   work

1 _____ company expenses every month to see where you spend money.
2 Location can make a big difference. Can you _____ to a cheaper office?
3 Turn lights and computers off to _____ energy.
4 Let your employees _____ remotely and you'll see better results.
5 _____ work to other people or companies if you can't hire more employees.
6 _____ tasks that are boring or that employees don't need to do.

Grammar

3 Write present sentences and questions using the prompts.
1 The item / be / out of stock / .
_____
2 Manufacturing / not take / a week / .
_____
3 They / not be / in the warehouse / .
_____
4 you / need / more time / ?
_____
5 He / need / a week / to build a custom model / .
_____
6 be / they / at a different factory / ?
_____

4 Complete the dialogue with the past form of the words in brackets.

A: What changes ¹_____ (you / make) at your company last year?
B: Let me see ... We ²_____ (hire) new employees, we ³_____ (upgrade) our technology, and the facilities department ⁴_____ (buy) new desks and chairs. The company ⁵_____ (not save) money but we ⁶_____ (improve) the office!
A: ⁷_____ (the employees / like) the changes?
B: Oh yes, absolutely! Also, management ⁸_____ (love) the changes because the company ⁹_____ (sell) more products last year as a result! Happy employees means better work!

5 Write the underlined verbs in the future. Use contractions if possible.

This project ¹improves the onboarding process at the company. It ²takes three months to complete but it ³doesn't start before April. Firstly, we ⁴have meetings with HR to discuss the onboarding process we have at the moment. Then, we ⁵hire an IT company and they ⁶upgrade the system. Finally, we ⁷check the new system works. The result is that new starters ⁸have a better experience.

1 _____*will improve*_____
2 _____
3 _____
4 _____
5 _____
6 _____
7 _____
8 _____

Functional language

6 Put the words in bold in the correct order.

I just want to say, ¹**happy very we're with** _we're very happy with_ the sales for this year – ²**job managing great** _____ the team, and ³**on selling done well** _____ in new countries. ⁴**that is The result** _____ we now have the most competitive product on the market. ⁵**talk future, In** _____ to Ben about marketing in different countries, and ⁶**to give try** _____ more presentations about the product. Well done!

Pronunciation bank

The sounds of English

These are the sounds of standard British English and American English pronunciation.

Consonants	
Symbol	Keyword
p	**p**en
b	**b**ack
t	**t**ea
d	**d**ay
k	**k**ey
g	**g**et
tʃ	**ch**urch
dʒ	**j**ob
f	**f**act
v	**v**ery
θ	**th**ing
ð	**th**is
s	**s**oon
z	**z**ero
ʃ	**sh**ip
ʒ	plea**s**ure
h	**h**ot
m	**m**ore
n	**n**ice
ŋ	thi**ng**
l	**l**ight
r	**r**ight
j	**y**ou
w	**w**ork

Vowels		
Symbol BrE	Symbol AmE	Keyword
ɪ	ɪ	k**i**t
e	e	dr**e**ss
æ	æ	b**a**d
ʌ	ʌ	b**u**t
ʊ	ʊ	f**oo**t
ɒ	ä	j**o**b
ə	ə	**a**bout
i	i	happ**y**
u	u	sit**u**ation
iː	i	f**ee**l
ɑː	ɑ	f**a**ther
ɔː	ɔ	n**or**th
uː	u	ch**oo**se
ɜː	ɚ	f**ir**st
eɪ	eɪ	d**ay**
aɪ	aɪ	pr**i**ce
ɔɪ	ɔɪ	b**oy**
əʊ	oʊ	n**o**
aʊ	aʊ	h**ow**
ɪə	ɪr	n**ear**
eə	er	h**air**
ʊə	ʊr	s**ure**

Pronunciation bank

Lesson 1.2
The alphabet

1A 🔊 P1.01 Listen and repeat.
1. A H J K
2. B C D E G P T V
3. F L M N S X Z
4. I Y
5. O
6. Q U W
7. R

B 🔊 P1.02 Work in pairs. Say the English alphabet in order. Then listen and check.
A, B, C, D, ...

2 🔊 P1.03 Listen and write the company names. Then work in pairs and practise saying them.
1. *DHL*
2. _____
3. _____
4. _____
5. _____
6. _____
7. _____
8. _____
9. _____
10. _____

3 🔊 P1.04 Listen and complete the names and addresses. Then work in pairs and practise saying them.
1. Ms _____
2. _____ @ _____ com
3. Nowak _____
4. _____ @hola _____
5. www _____
6. office _____

Lesson 1.3
Plural -s

1 🔊 P1.05 Listen and repeat.
/s/ /s/ /z/ /z/ /s/ /s/ /z/ /z/

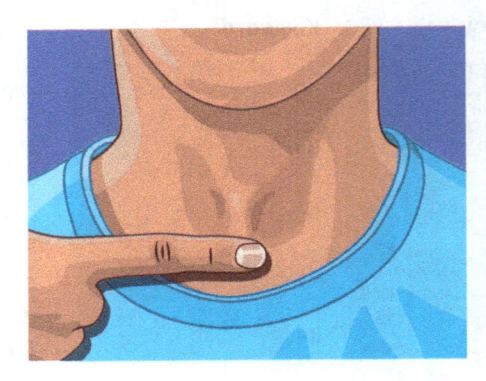

2 🔊 P1.06 Listen and repeat the plurals. Then work in pairs and practise saying the phrases.
1. shops /s/ and restaurants /s/
2. books /s/ for students /s/
3. employees /z/ at factories /z/
4. numbers /z/ and codes /z/

3A 🔊 P1.07 Listen to the phrases. The plurals here are different. Why?
1. your boss and our bosses /ɪz/
2. his office and their offices /ɪz/
3. my workplace and your workplaces /ɪz/
4. her address and our addresses /ɪz/

B Work in pairs. Practise saying the phrases in Exercise 3A.

4A Work in pairs. Look at the words in the box. Are the plurals with /s/, /z/ or /ɪz/?

| breaks buses jobs locations nights warehouses |

/s/ *breaks, ...* _____
/z/ _____
/ɪz/ _____

B 🔊 P1.08 Listen and check. Then practise saying the words.

Pronunciation bank

Lesson 2.2
Numbers

1 🔊 P2.01 **Listen and repeat.**

thirteen   thirty
fourteen   forty
fifteen   fifty
sixteen   sixty
seventeen seventy
eighteen   eighty
nineteen   ninety

2 🔊 P2.02 **Listen and underline the numbers you hear. Then listen again and repeat.**

1 *13 / 30* invoices
2 *13 / 30* projects
3 *14 / 40* thousand euros
4 *15 / 50* products
5 *16 / 60* employees
6 *17 / 70* customers
7 *18 / 80* million dollars
8 *19 / 90* cars

3 🔊 P2.03 **Listen to the dialogue. Then work in pairs and practise similar dialogues. Use the phrases in Exercise 2.**

A: *Is that thirteen or thirty invoices?*
B: *Thirty.*

4A **Work in pairs. Mark (∧) where you need to say *and* in these numbers.**

1 3∧14   *three hundred and fourteen*
2 977
3 8,239
4 33,414
5 432,746
6 7,950,110
7 13,800,514
8 423,049,113

B 🔊 P2.04 **Listen and check. Then work in pairs and practise saying the numbers in Exercise 4A.**

Lesson 2.3
Questions

1A 🔊 P2.05 **Listen and repeat.**

> do   do   does   does   do   do   does   does

B 🔊 P2.06 **Listen and repeat the questions. Start at the end.**

⬅

1 Where *do* you work?
2 What days *do* they work?
3 Where *does* he work?
4 What days *does* she work?

C 🔊 P2.07 **Listen to the questions. How do you pronounce *do* at the end? Why?**

1 What *do* you **do**?
2 What *do* they **do**?

2A 🔊 P2.08 **Listen to the questions. Do they go up (↑) at the end or down (↓)?**

1 *Do* you like your job? ↑
  What *do* you like about your job? ↓
2 *Do* they travel for work?
  How often *do* they travel for work?
3 *Does* it provide logistics services?
  What services *does* it provide?
4 *Does* your company sell products online?
  What *does* your company sell?

B **Work in pairs. Practise saying the questions in Exercise 2A.**

Pronunciation bank

Lesson 3.1
can and can't

1 🔊 P3.01 **Listen and repeat.**
I **can**! You **can't**! He **can**! She **can't**! It **can**!
We **can't**! You **can**! They **can't**!

2A 🔊 P3.02 **Listen to the questions. *Can* here is different. Why?**
1 **Can** you spell your name?
2 **Can** you speak French?
3 **Can** you design a website?
4 **Can** you manage a team?

B 🔊 P3.03 **Listen and repeat the questions in Exercise 2A.**
1 *Can you spell …*
   Can you spell your name?

C **Work in pairs. Ask each other the questions in Exercise 2A. Give short answers.**
  A: *Can you spell your name?*
  B: *Yes, I can.*

3A 🔊 P3.04 **Listen to the sentences. Is *can* stressed or unstressed? And *can't*?**
1 I **can** speak German but I **can't** speak Spanish.
2 She **can** work on Saturday but she **can't** work on Sunday.
3 We **can't** meet at 2 o'clock but we **can** meet at three.
4 They **can't** open in May but they **can** open in June.

B **Work in pairs. Practise saying the sentences in Exercise 3A.**

Lesson 3.2
Ordinal numbers

1A 🔊 P3.05 **Listen and repeat the numbers.**
My **fir**st name.   The **six**th in line.
The **second** number.   Your **seven**th day.
Her **thir**d visit.   His **eigh**th night.
The **four**th design.   The **nin**th copy.
The **fif**th floor.   The **ten**th month.

B 🔊 P3.06 **Now listen and repeat each line in Exercise 1A.**

2 🔊 P3.07 **Listen and repeat the numbers and dates.**
11**th** January   15**th** May   19**th** September
12**th** February   16**th** June   20**th** October
13**th** March   17**th** July   30**th** November
14**th** April   18**th** August   31**st** December

3A 🔊 P3.08 **Listen and ⊙circle⊙ the numbers you hear.**
1 *13th / 14th* August *2005 / 2015*
2 It's on the *14th / 40th* floor.
3 *11th / 12th* November *1918 / 1980*
4 It's his *30th / 40th* birthday.
5 It's their *15th / 50th* shop in the UK.
6 *13th / 30th* June *2013 / 2014*
7 It's their *17th / 70th* order.
8 *23rd / 24th* November *2019 / 2090*

B **Work in pairs. Practise saying the dates and sentences in Exercise 3A.**

Pronunciation bank

Lesson 4.1
The -ed ending

1 🔊 P4.01 Listen and repeat. The green past forms are different. Why?

ask	→	asked /t/
miss	→	missed /t/
plan	→	planned /d/
call	→	called /d/
want	→	wanted /ɪd/
end	→	ended /ɪd/

2A 🔊 P4.02 Listen and repeat the past forms.
1 It **worked** /t/ for two days and then it **stopped** /t/.
2 He **finished** /t/ his work and **helped** /t/ me.
3 She **phoned** /d/ me and **complained** /d/.
4 We **agreed** /d/ on a date but then they **changed** /d/ it.
5 We **started** /ɪd/ a company and **provided** /ɪd/ IT services.
6 They **needed** /ɪd/ my help and I **suggested** /ɪd/ a solution.

B 🔊 P4.03 Listen to the sentences in Exercise 2A. Then work in pairs and practise saying them.

3A 🔊 P4.04 Listen and tick (✓) the sentences you hear.
1 They **arrive** on time. ✓
  They **arrived** on time.
2 I **manage** a big team.
  I **managed** a big team.
3 We **fix** problems.
  We **fixed** problems.
4 They **accept** my offers.
  They **accepted** my offers.
5 We **talk** about the budget.
  We **talked** about the budget.
6 I **attend** all the meetings.
  I **attended** all the meetings.

B 🔊 P4.05 Listen and repeat the sentences in Exercise 3A. Are the past forms with /t/, /d/ or /ɪd/?

Lesson 4.3
'th' as /θ/ and /ð/

1A 🔊 P4.06 Listen and repeat.

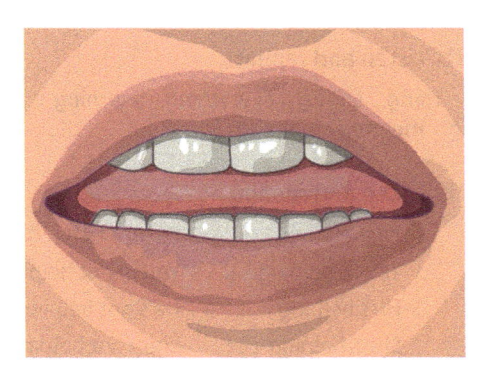

/θ/ /θ/   /ð/ /ð/   /θ/ /θ/   /ð/ /ð/

B Listen and repeat. Then work in pairs and practise saying the words.
🔊 P4.07 /θ/ thanks think thought nothing month birth
🔊 P4.08 /ð/ they this that there together with

2A 🔊 P4.09 Listen and repeat the words with th /θ/ and th /ð/.
1 He's free at three thirty on Thursday.
2 It's my fortieth birthday next month.
3 They talk about the weather every day.
4 We work together with the team.
5 Write to these clients in the UK and say thank you to them.
6 I thought the meeting in the Netherlands was on the thirteenth.

B 🔊 P4.10 Listen to the sentences in Exercise 2A. Then work in pairs and practise saying the sentences.

99

Pronunciation bank

Lesson 5.1
/ŋ/ and the Present Continuous

1A 🔊 P5.01 Listen and repeat. Point 👉 to where you **feel** the pronunciation of /ŋ/.

/ŋ/   /ŋ/   /ŋ/   /ŋ/   /ŋ/   /ŋ/

B 🔊 P5.02 Listen and repeat.

wro**ng**   thi**ng**   spri**ng**   everythi**ng**   morni**ng**
buildi**ng**   meeti**ng**   helpi**ng**

2 🔊 P5.03 Listen and repeat.

I'm	I'm helping.	I'm not helping.
You're	You're helping.	You're not helping.
He's	He's helping.	He's not helping.
She's	She's helping.	She's not helping.
It's	It's helping.	It's not helping.
We're	We're helping.	We're not helping.
They're	They're helping.	They're not helping.

3A 🔊 P5.04 Listen and repeat the *-ing* forms.

1 I'm **talking** to you but you're not **listening**.
2 He's **calling** her but she's not **answering**.
3 We're **having** a meeting but they're not **coming**.
4 I'm **pressing** the button but it's not **working**.
5 They're **selling** the company but we're not **buying** it.
6 We're **providing** new services but they're not **using** them.

B 🔊 P5.05 Listen to the sentences in Exercise 3A. Then work in pairs and practise saying them.

Lesson 5.3
/ɪ/ and /iː/

1 Listen and repeat the sounds /ɪ/ and /iː/ and the words.

🔊 P5.06 /ɪ/   f**i**x   pr**i**nt   **i**ll   g**i**ve   g**y**m   f**i**nish   m**i**nute   v**i**sit

🔊 P5.07 /iː/   k**ey**   b**ea**ch   sp**ea**k   f**ee**l   scr**ee**n   cant**ee**n   agr**ee**   coll**ea**gue

2 🔊 P5.08 Listen and repeat.

/ɪ/	→	/iː/
l**i**ve	→	l**ea**ve
f**i**ll	→	f**ee**l
T**i**m	→	t**ea**m
h**i**s	→	h**e**'s
s**i**t	→	s**ea**t

3A 🔊 P5.09 Listen and and ⓒircle the /ɪ/ sound(s) in the words in bold. Compare your answers with a partner.

1 My **colleague** is feeling **ill**.
2 **Tim's giving** your team **his greetings**.
3 I need to read the **minutes** of the **meeting**.
4 Can you **fix** the **machine this** week, please?
5 He's **leaving** the town to **live** near the beach.

B Listen again and underline the /iː/ sound(s) in the words in bold. Compare your answers with a partner.

1 My **colleague** is **feeling** ill.
2 Tim's giving your **team** his **greetings**.
3 I **need** to **read** the minutes of the **meeting**.
4 Can you fix the **machine** this **week**, **please**?
5 He's **leaving** the town to live near the **beach**.

C Practise saying the sentences in Exercise 3A.

Pronunciation bank

Lesson 6.1
The vowel /ə/

1 🔊 P6.01 Listen and repeat.

/ə/ /ə/

big	bigger
cheap	cheaper
long	longer
light	lighter
fast	faster
quiet	quieter
noisy	noisier
busy	busier

2 🔊 P6.02 Listen and repeat.

older than
shorter than
smaller than
easier than
happier than

3A 🔊 P6.03 Listen and repeat.
1 A train is faster than a car.
2 A conference is longer than a meeting.
3 A printer is cheaper than a computer.
4 The factory is older than the warehouse.
5 The task is easier than the project.
6 The manager is busier than the boss.

B Work in pairs. Practise saying the sentences in Exercise 3A.

Lesson 6.3
/æ/ and /ʌ/

1 Listen and repeat.

🔊 P6.04 /æ/ app back that bad brand have damaged manage package standard tablet relax

🔊 P6.05 /ʌ/ but cup much touch truck lunch button current country Monday summer discuss

2 🔊 P6.06 Listen and repeat.

/æ/	→	/ʌ/
app	→	up
bat	→	but
cap	→	cup
match	→	much
track	→	truck

3A 🔊 P6.07 Listen and circle the /æ/ sound(s) in the words in bold. Compare your answers with a partner.
1 We discussed the current **contract at** lunch.
2 See the **attachment** for the update on the budget.
3 I sent the broken **laptop back** to the shop on Monday.
4 Both the plus **package** and the **standard** offer free **national** calls.
5 If customers **have** problems with the **app**, they can **contact** me on this number.

B Listen and underline the /ʌ/ sound(s) in the other words in Exercise 3A. Compare your answers with a partner.

C Practise saying the sentences in Exercise 3A.

Pronunciation bank

Lesson 7.2
/aɪ/ and /eɪ/

1 Listen and repeat.
- P7.01 /aɪ/ my light nine sign type white item invite July online
- P7.02 /eɪ/ day great late make name train arrange explain create paper

2 P7.03 Listen and underline the word or words in each pair with /eɪ/.
1 app April
2 corporate celebrate
3 eight foreign
4 paid pay
5 said say
6 say says

3A P7.04 Listen to the sentences. Notice the /eɪ/ sounds and underline the /aɪ/ sounds.
1 We have to take five ring binders and a stapler.
2 Our clients complain that the website is complicated.
3 Why don't you write me an email with all the details?
4 The Sales Manager says there's a mistake in the final price.
5 They need more time to change the design.

B Compare with your partner. Then listen again and check. Practise saying the sentences in Exercise 3A.

Lesson 7.3
/l/ and /r/

1 Listen and repeat.
- P7.05 /l/ last left lunch lovely location black floor glass deadline tablet
- P7.06 /r/ rent room ready receive remove break free graph area sorry

2 P7.07 Listen and repeat.

/l/	→	/r/
lead	→	read
light	→	right
long	→	wrong
low	→	row
collect	→	correct

3 P7.08 Listen and repeat the underlined words.
1 We received the delivery on Friday at eleven.
2 The brown envelopes and the black pens arrived separately.
3 He's very friendly and polite to his colleagues.
4 Everything in the room was stylish and really excellent quality.
5 I'm free tomorrow so I'm going to visit my family and relax.

4 P7.09 Work in pairs and practise saying the sentences in Exercise 3.

Lesson 8.2
Pronouncing the letter 'o'

1 Listen and repeat the sounds /ɒ/ and /əʊ/ and the words.

🔊 P8.01 /ɒ/ off box job shop stock copy model offer project software

🔊 P8.02 /əʊ/ old clothes don't home phone hotel global Poland program total

2A 🔊 P8.03 Listen and circle the word in bold in each sentence with the /ɒ/ sound. Compare your answers with a partner.

1 We **relocated** to a new **office** last **month**.
2 The planning **process** didn't **cost** much **money**.
3 They **only** make this **product** in one **colour**.
4 I **love** your **conference photos**.
5 We **negotiated** new **contracts** with **other** suppliers.
6 The system **notifies** the **company** that there is a **problem**.

B Listen again and underline the word in bold in each sentence with the /əʊ/ sound in Exercise 2A. Compare your answers with a partner.

C Practise saying the sentences in Exercise 2A.

3 🔊 P8.04 Listen to the other words in bold in Exercise 2A. The letter 'o' is pronounced the same way in all of them. Is it ... ?

a /æ/ as in **a**pp
b /ʌ/ as in m**u**ch

Lesson 8.3
The vowel /ɜː/

1A 🔊 P8.05 Listen and repeat. What spellings represent the vowel /ɜː/?

/ɜː/   sir birth first confirm
turn further purchase Thursday
serve term commerce German

B 🔊 P8.06 We sometimes pronounce the letters 'or' as /ɜː/, but not always. Listen and underline the words with /ɜː/.

/ɜː/   form short word work world worse worst sorry worry information

C 🔊 P8.07 Listen and repeat the words with /ɜː/ from Exercise 1B.

2 🔊 P8.08 Listen and practise saying the sentences.

1 The payment **terms** are **worse** now.
2 They provide the **worst services** in the **world**!
3 For **further purchases** use the online form.
4 It's my **first** day at **work** after a short holiday.
5 We'll **confirm** the information on **Thursday**.
6 I **worked** for a **German e-commerce** company.

Irregular verbs list

	INFINITIVE	PAST SIMPLE		INFINITIVE	PAST SIMPLE
P9.01	be [bɪ:]	was/were [wɒz/wɜ:]	P9.24	let [let]	let [let]
P9.02	break [breɪk]	broke [brəʊk]	P9.25	lose [lu:z]	lost [lɒst]
P9.03	bring [brɪŋ]	brought [brɔ:t]	P9.26	make [meɪk]	made [meɪd]
P9.04	build [bɪld]	built [bɪlt]	P9.27	meet [mi:t]	met [met]
P9.05	buy [baɪ]	bought [bɔ:t]	P9.28	pay [peɪ]	paid [peɪd]
P9.06	can [kæn]	could [kʊd]	P9.29	put [pʊt]	put [pʊt]
P9.07	choose [tʃʊ:z]	chose [tʃəʊz]	P9.30	read [ri:d]	read [red]
P9.08	come [kʌm]	came [keɪm]	P9.31	ring [rɪŋ]	rang [ræŋ]
P9.09	cost [kɒst]	cost [kɒst]	P9.32	say [seɪ]	said [sed]
P9.10	cut [kʌt]	cut [kʌt]	P9.33	see [si:]	saw [sɔ:]
P9.11	do [dʊ:]	did [dɪd]	P9.34	sell [sel]	sold [səʊld]
P9.12	find [faɪnd]	found [faʊnd]	P9.35	send [send]	sent [sent]
P9.13	forget [fəˈget]	forgot [fəˈgɒt]	P9.36	show [ʃəʊ]	showed [ʃəʊd]
P9.14	get [get]	got [gɒt]	P9.37	speak [spi:k]	spoke [spəʊk]
P9.15	give [gɪv]	gave [geɪv]	P9.38	spell [spel]	spelt [spelt]/ spelled [speld]
P9.16	go [gəʊ]	went [went]	P9.39	spend [spend]	spent [spent]
P9.17	grow [grəʊ]	grew [gru:]	P9.40	take [teɪk]	took [tʊk]
P9.18	have [hæv]	had [hæd]	P9.41	teach [ti:tʃ]	taught [tɔ:t]
P9.19	hear [hɪə]	heard [hɜ:d]	P9.42	tell [tel]	told [təʊld]
P9.20	keep [ki:p]	kept [kept]	P9.43	think [θɪnk]	thought [θɔ:t]
P9.21	know [nəʊ]	knew [njʊ:]	P9.44	understand [ˌʌndəˈstænd]	understood [ˌʌndəˈstʊd]
P9.22	learn [lɜ:n]	learnt [lɜ:nt]/ learned [lɜ:nd]	P9.45	win [wɪn]	won [wʌn]
P9.23	leave [li:v]	left [left]	P9.46	write [raɪt]	wrote [rəʊt]

Grammar reference

1.1 Introductions: be

Positive

I	am/'m	
You/We/They	are/'re	German.
He/She/It	is/'s	from Germany.

Negative

I	am not/'m not	
You/We/They	are not/'re not/aren't	Polish.
He/She/It	is not/'s not/isn't	from Poland.

Yes/No questions

Am	I	
Are	you/we/they	Japanese?
Is	he/she/it	from Japan?

Short answers

	I	am.		I	'm not
Yes,	you/we/they	are.	No,	you/we/they	aren't.
	he/she/it	is.		he/she/it	isn't.

1 Complete the sentences with the words in the box.

> are   aren't   am   is   isn't (x2)   'm   not   're   's

1 **A:** _____ you from Japan?
  B: Yes, I _____ .
2 You are _____ from Poland.
3 He _____ British. He's American.
4 They _____ Mexican. They're from Argentina.
5 I _____ Spanish.
6 **A:** _____ she Chinese?
  B: No, she _____ .
7 We _____ not Indian.
8 It _____ from Ireland.

2 Match 1-4 with a-d and 5-8 with e-h.

1 I   a isn't from Spain.
2 My name   b 'm German.
3 She   c 're Mexican.
4 They   d 's Luis.

5 We   e is Ella.
6 David   f 'm not Japanese.
7 This   g 're from China.
8 I   h 's American.

1.2 my, your, his, her, its, our, their

1 Choose the correct word.

1 Call Mr Garcia. *Its / His / Their* phone number is 332 9909.
2 Email Mrs Jones. *Our / My / Her* email address is jones_emily@hemis.net.
3 **A:** What's *your / his / my* address?
  B: My address is 435 Grape Lane.
4 Call me. *Your / My / Their* mobile number is 334 9829.
5 Eva and Lise are German, but *their / his / her* company is Spanish.
6 We are from London. *Our / Your / Their* address is 29 Clark Street.
7 The hotel is in Manhattan. *Your / Its / My* name is Park Inn.
8 Maria is Mexican. *Her / Their / Its* surname is Sanchez.

1.3 Describing your company: there is/are

| There | is/'s | a one no | warehouse. |
| There | are | two five no restaurants. break rooms for employees. | offices. |

1 Choose the correct option.

1 There's _____ .
   a five factories
   b one warehouse.
   c no managers.
2 There are _____ .
   a warehouses in Germany.
   b a gym.
   c one office.
3 There is _____ .
   a factories in Turkey.
   b three warehouses in London.
   c an office in New York.
4 There's _____ .
   a no factories.
   b two divisions.
   c a Shipping Manager.

5 There are _____ .
   a an office.
   b canteens for employees.
   c no gym.
6 There is _____ .
   a one Sales Manager.
   b two employees.
   c no factories.
7 There's _____ .
   a a gym for employees.
   b three managers in Spain.
   c no offices in Japan.
8 There are _____ .
   a a sales department in the UK.
   b no warehouses.
   c one manager in Germany.

Grammar reference

2.1 Talking about work: Present Simple positive

Positive		
I/You/We/They	work	in the marketing department.
He/She/It	works	

Spelling rules for *he, she, it*

verb + -s		
He/She/It	checks	technical problems.
	makes	hybrid cars.

verb with consonant + -y → -ies.	
I/You/We/They	try.
He/She/It	tries.

irregular		
I/You/We/They	have	meetings.
He/She/It	has	
I/You/We/They	go	to the office.
He/She/It	goes	
I/You/We/They	do	reports.
He/She/It	does	

1 Choose the correct option.

1 He *work / works* on the computer.
2 She *have / has* meetings with other departments.
3 We *sell / sells* hybrid cars.
4 They *write / writes* reports.
5 I *manage / manages* a sales team.
6 You *work / works* for a French company.
7 It *make / makes* good coffee.
8 We *solve / solves* technical problems.
9 She *check / checks* the process is safe.
10 He *have / has* meetings with clients.

2.2 a/an

a + singular noun beginning with a <u>consonant sound</u>
a <u>c</u>ompany, **a** <u>w</u>arehouse
an + singular noun beginning with a <u>vowel sound</u>
an <u>a</u>irport, **an** <u>i</u>nternational company, **an** <u>h</u>our
no *a* or *an* with <u>plural nouns</u>
They are student<u>s</u>.

1 Complete the sentences with *a* or *an*.

1 She works for ____ Irish company.
2 He has ____ uniform.
3 Mendoza is ____ Argentinian city.
4 She is ____ engineer.
5 It is ____ factory.
6 I work in ____ café.
7 She works for ____ airline.
8 He is ____ Sales Manager.
9 They work for ____ e-commerce company.
10 The meeting is ____ hour.

2.3 Talking about routines: Present Simple negative and questions

Negative			
I/You/We/They	don't	work	for a Germany company.
He/She/It	doesn't		

Yes/No questions			
Do	I/you/we/they	work	for a Germany company?
Does	he/she/it		

Short answers					
Yes,	I/you/we/they	do.	No,	I/you/we/they	don't.
	he/she/it	does.		he/she/it	doesn't.

Open questions			
Where	do	I/you/we/they	work?
	does	he/she/it	
What	do	I/you/we/they	do?
	does	he/she/it	
What days	do	I/you/we/they	work?
	does	he/she/it	

1 Rewrite the negatives and questions with *she*.

1 What do you do?
   What does she do?
2 I don't work on Sunday.
   _____
3 Where do you live?
   _____
4 You don't have meetings.
   _____
5 What do you do at work?
   _____
6 They don't like the work.
   _____
7 What days do you work?
   _____
8 I don't work in the head office.
   _____
9 Do you travel for work?
   _____
10 We don't have a car.
    _____
11 Do you like the job?
    _____
12 You don't have a visa.
    _____

Grammar reference

2.4 Using 's and s'

singular noun + **'s**
to show possession
    Michael**'s** job
    the team**'s** work

plural noun + **'**
to show possession
    the employees**'** car park
    the managers**'** meeting

nouns with -s + **'** or **'s**
    Ross**'** office
    Ross**'s** office
    Agnes**'** team
    Agnes**'s** team

plural men and women + **'s**
    The men**'s** bathroom
    The women**'s** bathroom

1 Put *'s* or *s'* in the correct position. Put *'s* and *s'* if they are both correct.
1 the team **'s** work
2 two designer projects
3 James report
4 the marketing department meeting
5 Lucas mobile phone
6 the Sales Director parking space
7 the six manager offices
8 our customer emails

3.1 Talking about ability and possibility

Positive		
I/You/He/She/It/We/They	can	speak Chinese.

Negative		
I/You/He/She/It/We/They	can't cannot	speak Japanese.

Yes/No questions		
Can	I/you/he/she/it/we/they	speak German?

Short answers		
Yes,	I/you/he/she/it/we/they	can.
No,		can't.

Open questions			
When	can	I/you/he/she/it/we/they	finish?

Put the words in bold in the correct order.
1 I **go on can't** holiday in July.
    _____
2 **can I take** Monday off.
    _____
3 **take can't She** time off next week.
    _____
4 **go on can't they** holiday in April.
    _____
5 **can on go when you** holiday?
    _____

3.1 at, in, on, from … to …

Preposition	Example
at + • time • lunchtime, breakfast and the weekend • night	The meeting is **at** 9 a.m. Where do you eat **at** lunchtime? I never work **at** night.
in + • month • season • year • the morning, the afternoon and the evening (not night)	I'm free **in** June. The conference is **in** spring. The new contract starts **in** 2025. They don't work **in** the morning.
on + • day • date • special day • official holiday	The next workshop is **on** Friday. Our meeting is **on** 12th April. They are open **on** Valentine's Day. We're not open **on** New Year's Day.
from + day, time, date + **to** + day, time, date	We can deliver **from** Monday **to** Friday. They are open **from** 9 a.m. **to** 5 p.m. She is on holiday **from** 1st **to** 31st January.

1 Choose the correct option.
1 Are you open *at / on* 1st May?
2 We're open *from / to* 08.45 *from / to* 18.45.
3 The next meeting is *in / on* October, I think.
4 He's a Factory Manager but he doesn't work *in / at* night.
5 My busy months are *at / in* winter.
6 The company doesn't close *on / at* lunchtime.

3.2 Can … ?/Could … ?

Yes/No questions		
Can/Could	you	send me the report today, please?

Short answers		
Yes,	I/we	can.
No,		can't.

1 Write requests with *can* or *could*. Use the prompts.
1 I / take / time off / next week / ?
    Could I take time off next week?
2 we / meet / the clients / in your office / ?
    _____
3 she / call / me / this afternoon / ?
    _____
4 you / send / me / the details by email / ?
    _____
5 I / have / an extra day / to finish the report / ?
    _____
6 we / go for lunch early / today / please / ?
    _____

Grammar reference

3.3 Talking about the past

Positive		
I/He/She/It	was	late.
You/We/They	were	

Negative		
I/He/She/It	was not/wasn't	late.
You/We/They	were not/weren't	

Yes/No questions		
Was	I/he/she/it	late?
Were	you/we/they	

Short answers					
Yes,	I/he/she/it	was.	No,	I/he/she/it	wasn't.
	you/we/they	were.		you/we/they	weren't.

1 Complete the sentences with was(n't) or were(n't).
1 _____ there a problem with the order?
2 Where _____ they this afternoon?
3 A: There _____ ten items in the delivery, there _____ only eight.
  B: So, there are two items missing ...
4 _____ the product damaged? Or only the box?
5 _____ there any packages missing from your order?
6 Three people _____ late for our team meeting yesterday.
7 What time _____ the meeting? 2 p.m. or 3 p.m.?
8 A: _____ she late on Monday morning?
  B: No, she _____ .

4.1 Talking about the past: Past Simple

Positive		
I/You/He/She/It/We/They	verb + -ed **miss**ed	the meeting last week.
	verb with -e: + -d **arriv**ed	late yesterday.
	verb with consonant – vowel – consonant: consonant x2 + -ed **sto**pped	working at 5 p.m.
	verb with -y: → -ied **stud**ied	in Frankfurt.

See the irregular verbs list on page 104.

1 Rewrite the sentences in the past. The verbs are regular.
1 I study at Oxford.
  _____
2 My headphones stop working.
  _____
3 He manages a big team.
  _____
4 They miss the meeting.
  _____

2 Complete the sentences with the past form of the words in brackets. The verbs are irregular.
1 We _____ (make) a mistake.
2 You _____ (send) the delivery.
3 He _____ (give) me the report.
4 I _____ (write) the report yesterday.
5 They _____ (have) a meeting.
6 The train _____ (be) late.

4.2 Making offers and promises with will

I/You/He/She/It/We/They	will/'ll will not/won't	call you back. check the order.

1 Put the words in the correct order.
1 will / she / call you back
  _____
2 change the order now / I / will
  _____
3 they / check the database for you / will
  _____
4 will / send it by email / I
  _____
5 write the report / won't / we
  _____

4.3 Using negatives and questions in the past: Past Simple

Negative		
I/You/He/She/It/We/They	didn't	check the order. study in Paris. go to work.

Yes/No questions		
Did	I/you/he/she/it/we/they	finish the project? study in Australia? get the delivery?

Grammar reference

Open questions

What		the technician	say?
When	did	the delivery	arrive?
Where		I/you/he/she/it/we/they	buy it?

1 Complete the sentences with the negative past form of the words in the box.

come	go	have	manage	study

1 I _____ to work yesterday.
2 She _____ in New York.
3 I _____ the sales team.
4 We _____ a meeting.
5 The delivery _____ yesterday.

2 Complete the questions with the correct form of the words in brackets.

1 _____ (you / have) a meeting yesterday?
2 When _____ (the delivery / come)?
3 _____ (you / work) in Paris?
4 Where _____ (you / buy) it?
5 _____ (we / get) the order?

5.1 Talking about things happening now: Present Continuous

Positive

I	am/'m		now.
You/We/They	are/'re	working	right now.
He/She/It	is/'s		at the moment.

Negative

I	am not/'m not		now.
You/We/They	are not/'re not/aren't	working	right now.
He/She/It	is not/'s not/isn't		at the moment.

Spelling rules for -ing form

verb + -ing	
work	work**ing**
miss	miss**ing**
study	study**ing**

verb with -e → -ing	
writ~~e~~	writ**ing**
tak~~e~~	tak**ing**
mak~~e~~	mak**ing**

one-syllable and two-syllable verbs with the last syllable stressed and ending with consonant – vowel – consonant: → consonant x2 + -ing	
s**to**p	sto**pp**ing
s**i**t	si**tt**ing
be**gi**n	begi**nn**ing
pre**fe**r	prefe**rr**ing

Exceptions:

cancel → cancel**l**ing in BrE but cancel**i**ng in AmE
travel → travel**l**ing in BrE but travel**i**ng in AmE

1 Complete the sentences with the correct form of the words in brackets.

1 I _____ (write) a report right now.
2 They _____ (have) a meeting now.
3 We _____ (work) from home at the moment.
4 You _____ (wait) for a phone call right now.
5 He _____ (sit) at his desk at the moment.
6 She _____ (visit) a client right now.

2 Put the words in the correct order.

1 working / I'm / not / at / moment / the
   _____
2 having / not / we're / a / meeting / now / right
   _____
3 not / he's / a / client / visiting / now
   _____
4 not / they're / the / report / moment / writing / at / the
   _____
5 now / not / working / it's / right
   _____

5.3 Talking about future arrangements: Present Continuous

Yes/No questions

Am	I		tomorrow?
Are	you/we/they	meeting the client	on Monday? next week?
Is	he/she/it		next month?

Short answers

		I	am.		I	'm not
Yes,		you/we/they	are.	No,	you/we/they	aren't.
		he/she/it	is.		he/she/it	isn't.

1 Complete the questions about the future with the correct form of the words in brackets.

1 (we / have a meeting) on Monday?
   _____
2 (she / meet a client) next week?
   _____
3 (they / work from home) tomorrow?
   _____
4 (I / visit a supplier) next month?
   _____
5 (you / write the report) tomorrow?
   _____
6 (he / prepare the presentation slides) on Friday?
   _____

109

Grammar reference

6.1 Comparing two things

One syllable: + -er	cheap → cheaper small → smaller
Two syllables ending in -y: y → i + -er	busy → busier easy → easier
Two or more syllables: more	expensive → more expensive difficult → more difficult
Irregular	good → better bad → worse far → further
Adjectives ending consonant + vowel + consonant: final consonant x2 + -er	big → bigger

1 Use the information in the table to complete the sentences.

	Hamlin House	Tulio's
Price	$500 per month	$700 per month
Size	2,000 m²	1,500 m²
Distance from train station	200 m	500 m

Price
1 Hamlin House is _cheaper than_ Tulio's.
2 Tulio's is _____ Hamlin House.

Size
3 Hamlin House is _____ Tulio's.
4 Tulio's is _____ Hamlin House.

Distance from train station
5 Hamlin House is _____ Tulio's to the train station.
6 Tulio's is _____ Hamlin House from the train station.

6.2 good – better – best / bad – worse – worst

Irregular	good → better → best bad → worse → worst

1 Choose the correct option.
1 I like my new phone. It's very *better / good*.
2 This desk is *worst / worse* than the other one.
3 The payment terms are *better / more good* than the terms from other suppliers.
4 This is the *worst / baddest* product I bought.
5 The quality is very *bad / worse*.
6 I think it was the *better / best* product I used.

6.3 Making proposals with *if*

condition (*If* + Present Simple)	result (*will* + infinitive)
If we **choose** a cheaper offer,	we **will save** money.
If you **buy** more,	the unit price **will go** down.
If we **choose** the premium service,	we **will get** unlimited data.

1 Match 1–6 with a–f.
1 If you buy today,   a I'll get a better phone.
2 If I choose 'Premium plus', b the staff will be happier.
3 If we launch a new product, c you'll get a lower price.
4 If she buys from this company, d she'll have longer to pay.
5 If they buy standing desks, e it'll increase sales.
6 If he changes his provider, f he'll save money.

7.1 Talking about obligation: *have to*

Positive

I/You/We/They	have to	finish it.
He/She/It	has to	

Negative

I/You/We/They	don't	have to	finish it.
He/She/It	doesn't		

Yes/No questions

Do	I/you/we/they	have to	finish it?
Does	he/she/it		

Short answers

Yes,	I/you/we/they	do.
	he/she/it	does.
No,	I/you/we/they	don't.
	he/she/it	doesn't.

1 Complete the sentences with the positive or negative form of *have to*.
1 You _____ meet the client, but you can come if you want to.
2 He _____ finish the report by Friday. His boss needs it.
3 We _____ update the inventory every day. It's very important.
4 She _____ go to the meeting but it's OK if she wants to.

Grammar reference

2 Write questions with *have to* using the prompts.
1 he / see / the supplier / next week?
_____
2 they / work / late every day?
_____
3 you / visit / clients / every week?
_____
4 she / check / with the warehouse?
_____

3 Write short answers to the questions in Exercise b.
1 _____ (+)
2 _____ (−)
3 _____ (+)
4 _____ (−)

7.3 Writing instructions: Imperatives

Send	your invoice by email.
Don't give	us your bank details by email.
Confirm	your bank details with us by phone.
Remember / Don't forget	to check the invoice before you send it.

1 Write the sentences as imperatives. For one sentence there are two possible answers.
1 You need to send your invoice today.
   Send your invoice today.
2 Can you give us your bank details?
   _____
3 You can't send your bank details by email.
   _____
4 Will you change the printer ink cartridge?
   _____
5 You need to speak to the client today.
   _____
6 You should complete the report by tomorrow.
   _____
7 You need to remember to check the purchase orders.
   _____
8 Can you update the client on the project?
   _____

111

Numbers

🔊 P10.01

1	one
2	two
3	three
4	four
5	five
6	six
7	seven
8	eight
9	nine
10	ten
11	eleven
12	twelve
13	thirteen
14	fourteen
15	fifteen
16	sixteen
17	seventeen
18	eighteen
19	nineteen
20	twenty
21	twenty-one
22	twenty-two
23	twenty-three
24	twenty-four
25	twenty-five
26	twenty-six
27	twenty-seven
28	twenty-eight
29	twenty-nine
30	thirty
31	thirty-one
32	thirty-two
33	thirty-three
34	thirty-four
35	thirty-five

36	thirty-six
37	thirty-seven
38	thirty-eight
39	thirty-nine
40	forty
41	forty-one
42	forty-two
43	forty-three
44	forty-four
45	forty-five
46	forty-six
47	forty-seven
48	forty-eight
49	forty-nine
50	fifty
51	fifty-one
52	fifty-two
53	fifty-three
54	fifty-four
55	fifty-five
56	fifty-six
57	fifty-seven
58	fifty-eight
59	fifty-nine
60	sixty
61	sixty-one
62	sixty-two
63	sixty-three
64	sixty-four
65	sixty-five
66	sixty-six
67	sixty-seven
68	sixty-eight
69	sixty-nine
70	seventy

71	seventy-one
72	seventy-two
73	seventy-three
74	seventy-four
75	seventy-five
76	seventy-six
77	seventy-seven
78	seventy-eight
79	seventy-nine
80	eighty
81	eighty-one
82	eighty-two
83	eighty-three
84	eighty-four
85	eighty-five
86	eighty-six
87	eighty-seven
88	eighty-eight
89	eighty-nine
90	ninety
91	ninety-one
92	niney-two
93	ninety-three
94	ninety-four
95	ninety-five
96	ninety-six
97	ninety-seven
98	ninety-eight
99	ninety-nine
100	a/one hundred
1,000	a/one thousand
1,000,000	a/one million
1000,000,000	a/one billion

Additional material

BUSINESS WORKSHOP 1 ▶ 2B
Student A

1. You are the Human Resources Manager. Talk about the company.
   Company locations
   Head office (you are here): Bern, Switzerland
   Factory: Shenzen, China
   Warehouse: Hamburg, Germany

2. Now talk about the head office facilities.
   Head office facilities
   - employee break room
   - no gym
   - restaurants near office

BUSINESS WORKSHOP 1 ▶ 2C
Student B

1. You are the new employee. Listen to the Human Resources Manager's description of the company. Match 1–3 with a–c.
   1. Head office   a Dublin, Ireland
   2. Factory   b Hong Kong
   3. Warehouse   c Krakow, Poland

2. Listen to Student A. Tick (✓) the facilities that your workplace has.
   Head office facilities
   - employee break room
   - canteen
   - restaurants near office
   - gym

BUSINESS WORKSHOP 3 ▶ 2
Student B

Work with another Student B. Put the bold words in the correct order.

1. **were with problems there** their last three orders.
   _____
2. **need change to we** how the warehouse works.
   _____
3. We often **problems with have** this delivery company.
   _____
4. **look for can we** a different delivery company.
   _____
5. **I can we think** find a solution by Friday.
   _____
6. **can we meet them** to tell them about the solutions. Can you come with me?
   _____

Read your rolecard and prepare for the meeting with your manager.

> You are a Sales Representative at Denilson's. GKB Production is your client.
> Meet your manager.
> Discuss the delivery problems with him/her.
> Use the agenda and try to include the sentences above in your conversation.
> Agree on possible solutions and a time to visit GKB together.

Work in Student A/B pairs. Have the meeting.

AGENDA
1. Discuss the <u>problems</u> with the GKB delivery.
2. Discuss possible <u>solutions</u>.

Lesson 3.4 ▶ 4
Student B

You are the Product Designer.

Answer the Production Manager's (Student A's) questions about the new car design.
- design not finished
- problem – the electronics design
- solution – do more tests
- on schedule

We aren't finished.
There was a problem with …

Lesson 3.2 ▶ 5
Student B

10	16	13
1	30	19

> Additional material

Lesson 2.2 ▶ 9B

Student A

Company name	Dell
Business	sells computers and electronics
Head office	Round Rock, Texas, USA
Countries	182
Staff	approximately 102,000

Lesson 4.1 ▶ 6B

Student A

Use the notes to tell a story about a problem at work.

- I / have a business trip
- My train / be late / so I / miss the meeting
- I / call the client / and I / say sorry
- I / explain the problem / to my manager

Lesson 6.2 ▶ 5A

Student A

The Work Furniture Specialist

Meeting chair quote

Hi Lidia,

Thank you for your email. Here's a summary of our quote:

  Product Name: Milan office chair
  Unit price: $90.00
  Minimum order: 15 units
  Delivery time: 20 days
  Payment terms: 60 days

Let me know if you need anything else. I am available via email or you can call any time on 202 555 0126.

Best,
Kay Fowler
Sales Representative
The Work Furniture Specialist

Lesson 2.1 ▶ 6A

Student A

Name: Pawel/Paula Nowak
City/Country: Krakow, Poland
Company/Department: international hotel chain
Job: Hotel Manager
Responsibilities: ten staff, emails, phone calls, guest problems

Lesson 4.2 ▶ 8

Student A

Phone calls 1 and 2 – You want to talk to Student C, but Student B answers your call.

- You are the Supplies Manager at Mantala Engineering.
- An important delivery is late.
- Phone your contact at the delivery company (Student C).
- Ask when the delivery will arrive.

Phone calls 3 and 4 – Student C gives you a message from Student B. Read the message and call Student A.

- You are the Office Supplies Manager at Foster Newman's, a retail company.
- Student C gave you some notes about a call from the Head of Finance (Student B).
- Phone Student B and offer a solution to the problem.

(Possible solutions:

- offer to ask the supplier when they will deliver the ink
- offer to give finance some ink from your department)

Phone calls 5 and 6 – Student C wants to talk to Student B, but you answer the call.

- You are a Sales Representative for BGS Supplies.
- A customer (Student C) will call and ask to speak to your colleague (Student B).
- Explain that Student B is not free and say why (in a meeting / at lunch / on the phone).
- Ask about the problem and take notes.
- After the call, give the notes to Student B.

Lesson 3.2 ▶ 9

Student A

Phone call 1

You are an employee. You want to go on holiday on Tuesday, Wednesday and Thursday next week. Phone your manager (Student B) to ask for the three days.

Student B: Good morning. Sonia Hein speaking. How can I help you?
Student A: Hi, Sonia, it's Lucas.
Student B: Hi, Lucas. How are you?
Student A: I'm good thanks. Can I … ?

Student A: Bye, Lucas.
Student B: Thank you! See you later!

Phone call 2

You are a manager. Your employee (Student B) wants to go on holiday this week and next. There are three people on holiday next week. Student B can't go on holiday then. Ask Student B if he/she can take two or three days' holiday this week.

Additional material

Lesson 2.2 > 9B
Student B

Company name	Inditex
Business	sells clothes
Head office	Arteixo (A Coruña), Spain
Countries	96
Staff	approximately 174,386

BUSINESS WORKSHOP 1 > 2B
Student B

1 You are the new employee. Listen to the Human Resources Manager's description of the company. Match 1–3 with a–c.
1 Head office
2 Factory
3 Warehouse
a Shenzen, China
b Bern, Switzerland
c Hamburg, Germany

2 Listen to Student A. Tick (✓) the facilities that your workplace has.

Head office facilities
- employee break room
- small canteen
- gym
- restaurants near office

BUSINESS WORKSHOP 3 > 3
Student B

You are the Sales Representative at Denilson's. You and your manager have a meeting with GKB on Monday 12th May to say sorry for the problems and to explain solutions.

You need a day off on Monday 12th May because of a family problem.

Phone your manager and use the information below in your call.
- Ask your manager for a 'personal day' on Monday 12th May.
- Check your boss knows that the meeting is at 10 a.m. on Monday 12th May.
- Tell your boss you can give him/her information about the new delivery company on Thursday 8th May.

BUSINESS WORKSHOP 1 > 2C
Student A

1 You are the Human Resources Manager. Talk about the company.

Company locations
Head office (you are here): Krakow, Poland
Factory: Hong Kong
Warehouse: Dublin, Ireland

2 Now talk about the head office facilities.

Head office facilities
- canteen
- no restaurants near office
- gym

Lesson 3.4 > 4
Student C

You are the Purchasing Manager.

Answer the Production Manager's (Student A's) questions about the supplier.
- not happy with our supplier
- problem – lots of broken/damaged parts
- solution – find a different supplier
- need more time

The problem is …
I think we can …

Lesson 4.3 > 7

Broken washing machine
B.Melinsa <B.Melinsa_3@Pmail.com>

Dear Sir/Madam,

I am writing to complain about a washing machine I bought last week.

Unfortunately, when I wanted to use the machine for the first time the door didn't close. There was some tape covering the lock. Then, the machine didn't start. A little button that looked like a lock flashed. So I couldn't use it.

I would like a new washing machine, please.

Best regards,

Barbara Melinsa

Additional material

Lesson 2.1 ▶ 6A

Student B
Name: Hans/Hannah Müller
City/Country: Leipzig, Germany
Company/Department: import/export, sales
Job: Sales Representative
Responsibilities: phone calls, emails, meetings with clients, sales reports

Lesson 4.2 ▶ 8

Student B

Phone calls 1 and 2 – Student A wants to talk to Student C, but you answer the call.

- You are a Customer Service Assistant at AGTN Logistics, a delivery company.
- A customer (Student A) will call and ask to speak to your colleague (Student C).
- Explain that Student C is not free and say why (in a meeting / at lunch / on the phone).
- Ask about the problem and take notes.
- After the call, give the notes to Student C.

Phone calls 3 and 4 – You want to talk to Student A, but Student C answers your call.

- You are the Head of Finance at Foster Newman's, a retail company.
- Your department doesn't have any ink for the printer.
- Phone the Office Supplies Manager in the purchasing department (Student A).
- Ask when the ink will arrive.

Phone calls 5 and 6 – Student A gives you a message from Student C. Read the message and call Student A.

- You are a Sales Representative for BGS Supplies.
- Student A gave you some notes about a call from a customer (Student C).
- Phone Student C and offer a solution to the problem.
(Possible solutions:
- change the date
- send new invoice)

Lesson 8.3 ▶ 6

NOTES:

Reduce the lead time for our computers

Time to complete: six months – the deadline is April next year
1 negotiate with the supplier – reduce the production time
2 use more warehouses – reduce the shipping time
3 hire more employees

Result: more competitive

Lesson 3.2 ▶ 5

Student C

50	10	60
16	13	90

Lesson 5.2 ▶ 7

Student A

Phone call 1

- You are working with your colleague (Student B) on a new project.
- Look at your calendar and add another three-hour meeting.
- Phone Student B to arrange a meeting to discuss the project. You need two hours.

B: *Are you free on Monday morning?*
A: *Sorry, I have a meeting from nine to twelve. I'm free on …*

	Monday	Tuesday	Wednesday	Thursday	Friday
9 a.m.–10 a.m.			Meeting	Meeting	
10 a.m.–11 a.m.	Meeting	Meeting			Meeting
11 a.m.–12 a.m.					
12 a.m.–1 p.m.		Lunch		Lunch	Lunch
1 p.m.–2 p.m.		Lunch			Lunch with clients
2 p.m.–3 p.m.					
3 p.m.–4 p.m.	Presentation	Phone call			
4 p.m.–5 p.m.					

Phone call 2

- You have an important meeting and can't meet your colleague.
- Phone Student B and ask to postpone the meeting.
- Use the diary to find a new time to meet.
- Remember you need two hours.

A: *… Listen. I'm afraid I need to postpone our meeting on … I have another appointment.*
B: *OK, that's not a problem. I'm free on …*

Lesson 6.2 ▶ 5A

Student D
What's the product name?
What's the unit price?
What's the minimum order?
What's the delivery time?
What are the payment terms?

Additional material

Lesson 4.4 ▶ 6

Student B

Scenario 1

You work in an electronics shop. A customer (Student A) will come in with a problem.

Listen to his/her problem and use the notes to help him/her.

Read the notes and think about what you can say.

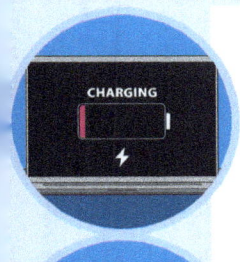

- Listen to the customer's problem.
- Ask the customer if he/she tried charging the laptop.
- Ask the customer if he/she took the battery out.
- Tell the customer that you can:
  – give him/her his/her money back.
  – give him/her a different laptop.
  – order a new one.
- Listen to the customer's choice.
- Tell the customer what you will do next.

Scenario 2

You just bought a new phone. When you got home, the volume control didn't work. Take it back to the shop and explain the problem to the Sales Assistant (Student A).

Read the notes and think about what you can say.

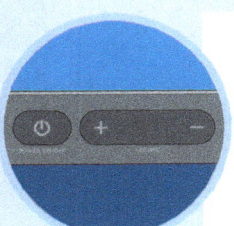

- Bought the phone yesterday.
- Volume doesn't work.
- Tried turning it off and on.
- Tried cleaning the volume button.
- Didn't help.
- Listen to the Sales Assistant's options.
- Make a decision about what you prefer.

Lesson 3.4 ▶ 4

Student D

You are the Marketing Manager.

Answer the Production Manager's (Student A's) questions about the website.

- website not finished
- problem – missing price information
- solution – ask sales for a new price list to give to the website designer
- on schedule

It isn't finished.
There's a problem with ...

BUSINESS WORKSHOP 4 ▶ 1

Student B

Read the information. Then answer Student A's call.

- You work for PTC Supplies.
- A customer will call you with a problem.
- Answer the call, listen to the problem and take notes.
- Say you will send a replacement the next day.

Answering a phone call
Hello, (your company).
This is (your name).
How can I help you?
I'm sorry about that.
Can I take the order number?
I can send ... tomorrow / next week.
I'll send ... tomorrow / next week.
Can I help you with anything else?

Lesson 5.2 ▶ 7

Student B

Phone call 1

- You are working with your colleague (Student A) on a new project.
- Look at your calendar and add another three-hour meeting.
- Student A will phone you to arrange a meeting to discuss the project. You need two hours.

A: *Are you free on Monday afternoon?*
B: *Sorry, I have a meeting from two to five. I'm free on ...*

	Monday	Tuesday	Wednesday	Thursday	Friday
9 a.m.–10 a.m.		Meeting	Meeting		
10 a.m.–11 a.m.				Meeting	Meeting
11 a.m.–12 a.m.					
12 a.m.–1 p.m.	Lunch		Lunch	Lunch	
1 p.m.–2 p.m.		Lunch			Meeting
2 p.m.–3 p.m.			Presentation		
3 p.m.–4 p.m.	Meeting	Meeting		Meeting	
4 p.m.–5 p.m.					

Phone call 2

- Student A will phone you to postpone your meeting.
- Use the diary to find a new time to meet.
- Remember you need two hours.

A: *... Listen. I'm afraid I need to postpone our meeting on ...*
I have another appointment.
B: *OK, that's not a problem. I'm free on ...*

Additional material

Lesson 4.2 ▶ 8

Student C

Phone calls 1 and 2 – Student B gives you a message from Student A. Read the message and call Student A.

- You are a Customer Service Assistant at AGTN Logistics, a delivery company.
- Student B gave you some notes about a call from the Supplies Manager at Mantala Engineering (Student A).
- Phone Student A and offer a solution to the problem.

(Possible solution:
- offer to call the driver and ask when he/she will deliver the item)

Phone calls 3 and 4 – Student B wants to talk to Student A, but you answer the call.

- You work in purchasing at Foster Newman's, a retail company.
- The Head of Finance (Student B) will call to speak to the Office Supplies Manager (Student A).
- Explain that Student A is not free and say why (in a meeting / at lunch / on the phone).
- Ask about the problem and take notes.
- When you have written the notes, give the notes to Student A.

Phone calls 5 and 6 – You want to talk to Student B, but Student A answers your call.

- You work in purchasing at CTG, a manufacturing company.
- The date on your invoice from a supplier, BGS Supplies, is wrong.
- Phone your contact at BGS Supplies (Student B).
- Explain the problem.

BUSINESS WORKSHOP 7 ▶ 2

Student B

You are the Supply Office Manager.

You think the company should buy a new IT system to order parts.

With the new system:
- The Production Manager can complete a form online to order the part.
- The system tells the supply office and finance about the order.
- The supply office can order the part online.
- The system tells the supply office and Production Manager when the part will arrive.

I think we should …
Why not …
Why don't we …
It's good because …

Lesson 3.2 ▶ 5

Student D

13	1	30
15	19	60

Lesson 6.2 ▶ 5A

Student B

Brench Office Supplies

Chair quote

Dear Ms Sandeo,

Thank you for your interest in our products. Please find a summary of our offer below:

   Product Name: Benson meeting chair

   Unit price: $75.50

   Minimum order: 20 units

   Delivery time: 30 days

   Payment terms: 30 days

Please contact me via email or phone on 202 555 0145 if you would like to place an order.

Best regards,

Tim Davidson
Sales Representative
Brench Office Supplies

Lesson 7.1 ▶ 7

Student A

Task 1

Use the information to tell your partner how to create a new purchase order.

- have / go into / the system
- have / choose / 'Create purchase order'
- have / enter / the details into the system
- not have / notify / the supplier
- your manager / have / approve the purchase order
- when you receive the items / have / request an invoice from the supplier
- have / check / the invoice
- have / approve payment

Task 2

Listen to your partner explain how to create a new invoice. Write down the steps. Ask questions if you don't understand.

Additional material

BUSINESS WORKSHOP 6 — 2A
Student B

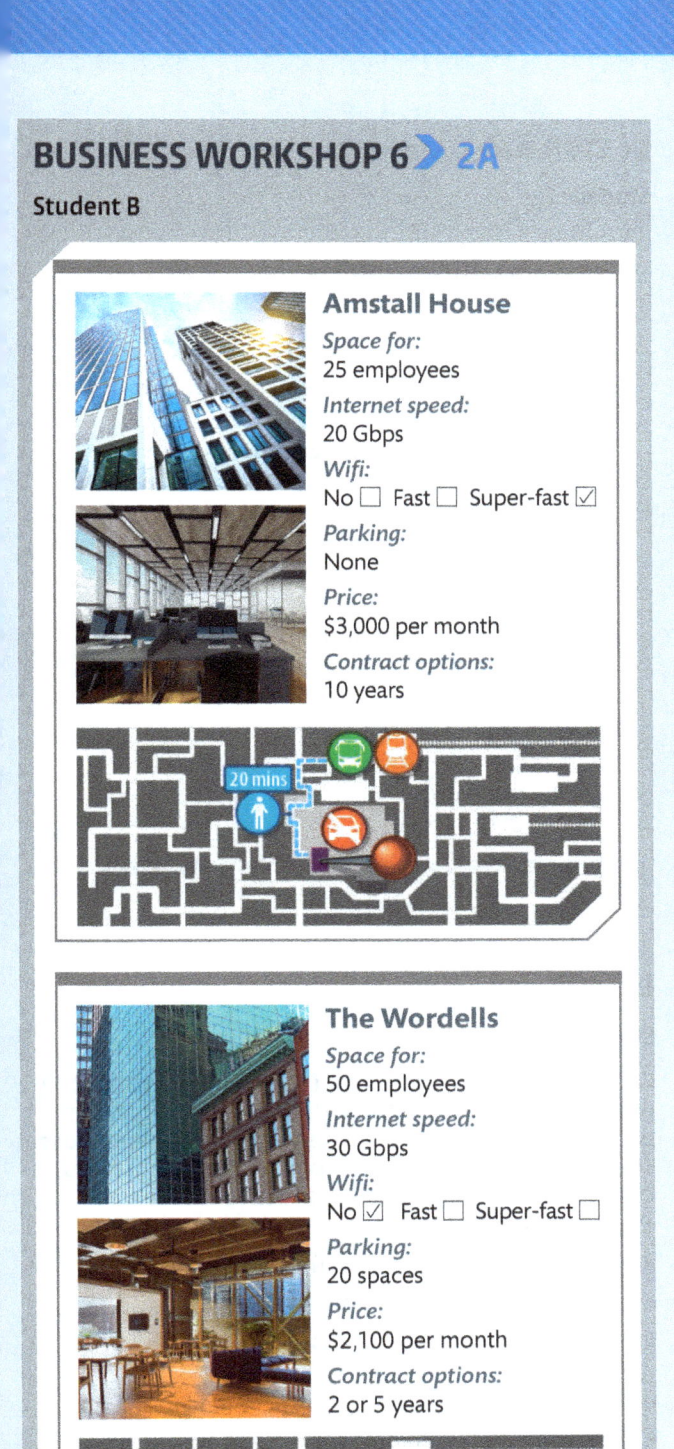

Amstall House
Space for: 25 employees
Internet speed: 20 Gbps
Wifi: No ☐ Fast ☐ Super-fast ☑
Parking: None
Price: $3,000 per month
Contract options: 10 years

The Wordells
Space for: 50 employees
Internet speed: 30 Gbps
Wifi: No ☑ Fast ☐ Super-fast ☐
Parking: 20 spaces
Price: $2,100 per month
Contract options: 2 or 5 years

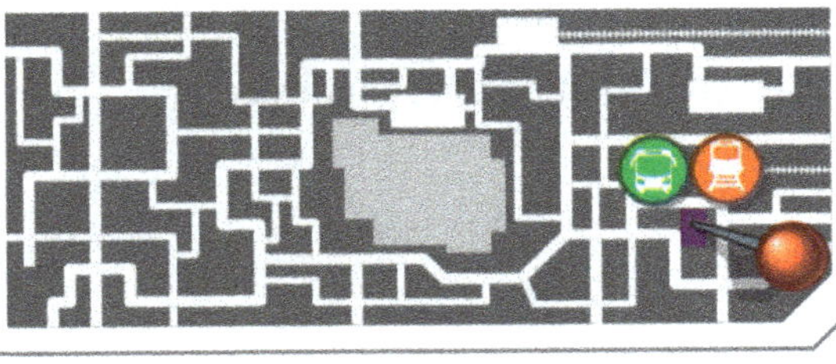

Amstall House is closer than The Wordells to the city centre.

Lesson 6.4 — 5A
Student B

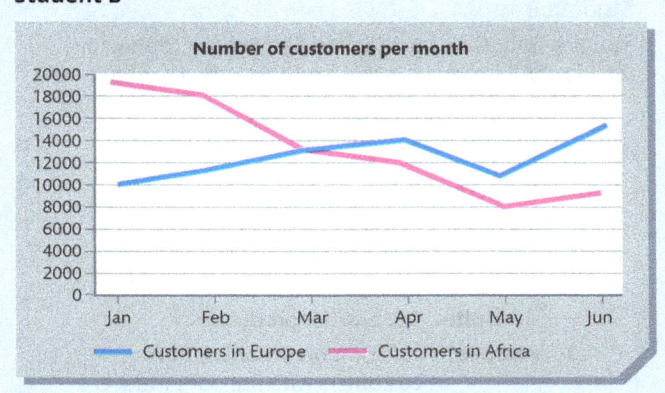

Number of customers per month (line graph: Customers in Europe, Customers in Africa; Jan–Jun)

The slide shows a ¹l___ g____ of our customers in Europe and in Africa. As you ²c__ s__ from the line graph, the number of customers in Europe was higher in June than in January. Now, let's ³l___ a_ the customers in Africa. As you can see on the ⁴s____, the number of customers in Africa was lower in June than in January. May was a bad month for both Europe and Africa. But, if you look at June, ⁵you'__ s__ that the number of customers in Africa and Europe was higher than in May.

Lesson 3.2 — 9
Student B

Phone call 1
You are a manager. Your employee (Student A) wants to go on holiday next week. The team is very busy next week. Student A can only take one day of holiday then. If he/she wants more time, ask him/her if he/she can go on holiday in two weeks.

Student B
- Good morning. Sonia Hein speaking. How can I help you?
- Hi, Lucas. How are you?
- Bye, Lucas.

Student A
- Hi, Sonia, it's Lucas.
- I'm good thanks. Can I … ?
- Thank you! See you later!

Phone call 2
You are an employee. You want to go on holiday on Friday this week and Monday next week. Phone your manager (Student A) to ask for the two days.

Lesson 3.4 — 4
Student A

You are the Production Manager. Ask:
1 Student B (the Product Designer) about the new car design.
2 Student C (the Purchasing Manager) about the supplier.
3 Student D (the Marketing Manager) about the website.

For each point, ask your colleague about:
Progress → Problems and solutions → Schedule

Additional material

BUSINESS WORKSHOP 8 ▶ 3

Student B

You are Tom. Give feedback to Sam, your employee (Student A). Read the notes and think about what you can say.

Project:	Improving the product design
Positives:	Upgrade the processor and software on the X290
	Change the product materials
Result:	Sell a better product
To improve:	Ask for more feedback from customers who use our products
	Attend all meetings

Lesson 8.4 ▶ 5

Student B

You work for Mitrello, a sales company. Read the notes and think about what you can say. Then give feedback to your employee (Student A).

Project:	Upgrading the company's technology
Positives:	Listen to the employees
	Solve the technical problems
Result:	The IT system in the office is better
To improve:	Save more money
	Communicate with the team every week

BUSINESS WORKSHOP 7 ▶ 2

Student C

You are the Finance Manager.

You agree the company should buy a new IT system to order parts.

With the new system:

- Finance can approve payments online.
- The system tells the supply office that finance approved a payment.
- The system tells the Production Manager when the supply office order the part.
- The system saves all documents automatically.

I think we should …
Why not …
Why don't we …
It's good because …

Lesson 6.2 ▶ 5A

Student C

Winners Office Supplies

<u>Supply offer</u>

Dear Ms Sandeo,

In response to your email, please find a summary of our offer below:

- Product Name: Soldero meeting chair
- Unit price: $50.00
- Minimum order: 10 units
- Delivery time: 60 days
- Payment terms: 90 days

Please contact me by email or on 202 555 0120 if you would like to place an order or if you need further assistance.

Best regards,

Karl Peterson
Sales Representative
Winners Office Supplies

Lesson 7.2 ▶ 7A

Student A

Your company has a problem. The inventory system only updates on Thursdays. When the sales team accept an order they don't know if the items are in the warehouse. The warehouse team cannot complete large orders so customers don't receive items or deliveries are late.

1 Put the steps of the solution in the correct order.

a Sales receive the order and enter it on the system. ____
b Sales confirm with the client the order and delivery date. ____
c Warehouse confirm with sales what items they will ship and when. ____
d Sales check with the warehouse that the product is in stock. ____
e The client receives the order. ____

2 Explain your solution to your partner.

Lesson 8.1 ▶ 8

Student A

Explain the information on the database to Student B.

Rentuno 450 – custom model	
In stock? (✓/✗):	✗
Manufacturing:	2.5 weeks
Shipping:	6 weeks
Inspection:	1–2 working days
Lead time:	9 weeks

Additional material

Lesson 8.1 > 8

Student B
Explain the information on the database to Student A.

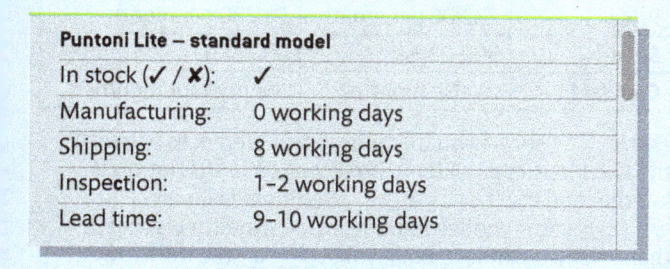

Puntoni Lite — standard model	
In stock (✓ / ✗):	✓
Manufacturing:	0 working days
Shipping:	8 working days
Inspection:	1–2 working days
Lead time:	9–10 working days

BUSINESS WORKSHOP 6 > 2A

Student A

1A Foster Street

Space for:	up to 30 employees
Internet speed:	25 Gbps
Wifi:	No ☐ Fast ☐ Super-fast ☑
Parking:	250 spaces
Price:	$2,450 per month
Contract options:	2, 3 or 5 years

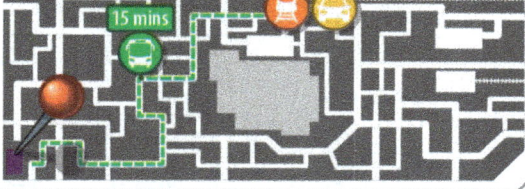

Berlin House

Space for:	40 employees
Internet speed:	15 Gbps
Wifi:	No ☑ Fast ☐ Super-fast ☐
Parking:	None
Price:	$1,850 per month
Contract options:	1, 2, 5 or 10 years

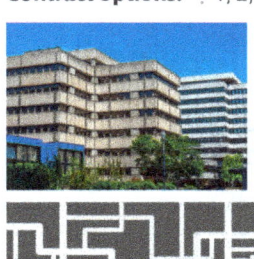

Berlin House is bigger than 1A Foster Street.

Lesson 7.2 > 7A

Student B

Your company has a problem. The inventory system only updates on Thursdays. When the sales team accept an order they don't know if the items are in the warehouse. The warehouse team cannot complete large orders so customers don't receive items or deliveries are late.

1 Complete the stages with the words in the box.

| confirm   have   inventory   receive   update |

1 Change the _____ system to a new one.
2 The inventory has to _____ every twelve hours.
3 Sales don't _____ to check stock with the warehouse.
4 Sales check inventory on the system and can _____ orders with clients.
5 Clients _____ orders on time.

2 Explain your solution to your partner.

Lesson 7.1 > 7

Student B

Task 1

Listen to your partner explain how to create a new purchase order. Write down the steps. Ask questions if you don't understand.

Task 2

Use the information to tell your partner how to create a new invoice.

- have / go into / the system
- have / choose / 'Create invoice'
- salesperson / have / request the invoice
- have / enter / the customer details
- have / put / a purchase order number on the invoice
- have / enter / the invoice on the customer's system
- not have / notify / the customer
- the customer / have / approve the invoice

BUSINESS WORKSHOP 8 > 3

Student A

You are Tom. Give feedback to Alex, your employee (Student B). Read the notes and think about what you can say.

Project:	Improving the supply chain
Positives:	Negotiate with the suppliers in Poland
	Find a new warehouse for Central Europe
Result:	The Managing Director in Rotterdam is very happy
To improve:	Communicate more with finance
	Ask for help if you need it

Additional material

BUSINESS WORKSHOP 2 > 5

Invent a new identity. Choose one item from each section of the table or use your own ideas.

Name	• Daniel/Daniela • Karl/Karla • Martin/Martina • other
Surname	• Smith • Hein • Casas • other
Home town	• Washington • Stuttgart • Buenos Aires • other
Nationality	• American • German • Argentinian • other
Based in	• Paris, France • Poznań, Poland • Tokyo, Japan • other
Company	• e-commerce – sells clothes and shoes online • car manufacturer – designs, makes and sells cars • pharmaceutical company – makes and sells pharmaceutical products • other
Job	• IT Specialist – work on IT projects; design and update software; solve technical problems • Finance Manager – manage a team; have meetings with other departments; write financial reports • Sales Manager – manage sales team; have meetings with clients; write sales reports • other
Travel for work	• two or three conferences a year in Europe • every month – Germany, France and all over Europe • every three months – go to the head office in the USA • other

Imagine everyone in the class is at an international conference. Follow these steps.

- Walk around the room.
- Meet people at the conference.
- Introduce yourself.
- Ask and answer questions about your jobs and companies.
- Say goodbye and talk to another person at the conference.

Lesson 4.1 > 6B

Student B

Use the notes to tell a story about a problem at work.
- I / have a meeting / with a client
- I / write the wrong time
- I / go to the meeting / but I / be very late
- I / miss the meeting / so I / say sorry to the client

Lesson 6.4 > 5A

Student A

	Intranui Internet	Priomea Connect
Price	£3,900 per month	£4,250 per month
Speed	300 Gbps	500 Gbps
Contract	twelve months	twenty-four months

This ^{1}t _ _ _ _ shows you the three main differences between the two internet providers. The second column is Intranui Internet and the ^{2}t _ _ _ _ c _ _ _ _ _ is Priomea Connect. As ^{3}y _ _ c _ _ see in the second row, Intranui Internet is cheaper than Priomea Connect. But if you ^{4}l _ _ _ a _ the third row, you'll see that Priomea Connect is faster than Intranui Internet. Now, let's look at the contract. If you look at the fourth row, ^{5}you' _ _ s _ _ that Intranui Internet's contract is shorter than Priomea Connect's contract.

Lesson 7.1 > 1

Match 1–5 with a–e.

1 The purchase order is from
2 The invoice is from
3 The PO says what
4 The invoice says what
5 Mark Smith created

a Total Office World to KDTX plc.
b KDTX ordered from Total Office World
c the purchase order.
d KDTX plc to Total Office World.
e Total Office World delivered to KDTX

KDTX plc

NOTTINGHAM OFFICE, TALBOT ST, NOTTINGHAM, NG1 5

PURCHASE ORDER

PO number: PO120034	04/01/2020

Supplier	Delivery address
Total Office World Unit 13, Trent Lane Retail Park Nottingham, NG4 2HN	Nottingham office Talbot St Nottingham NG1 5FD Attn: Mark Smith

Delivery date	Requested by	Approved by	Department
10/01/2020	Mark Smith	Mark Smith	admin

Notes
Office supplies Q1

Item name	Item code	Quantity	Item price	Total
ink	qdt-2340	10	8.99	89.90
A4 paper	PPR542	10	12.99	129.99

Total Office World
Unit 13, Trent Lane Retail Park, Nottingham, NG4 2HN

Invoice No:	123/01/2020a
Invoice Date:	10/01/2020
Payment terms:	30 days from date of invoice by bank transfer

PO number: PO120034

Invoice For:

ITEM NAME	ITEM CODE	QTY.	ITEM PRICE	TOTAL
ink	qdt-2340	10	8.99	89.90
A4 paper	PPR542	10	12.99	129.99

Videoscripts

1.1.1
Part 1
I = Interviewer   Y = Yumiko
- I: Hello.
- Y: Hello.
- I: What's your name?
- Y: My name is Yumiko.
- I: Where are you from?
- Y: I am from Tokyo in Japan.
- I: What's your nationality?
- Y: I am Japanese.
- I: What's your job?
- Y: I am an Admin Assistant.
- I: Nice to meet you.
- Y: Nice to meet you, too.

Part 2
I = Interviewer   J = Jan   G = Gosia
- I: Hello!
- J: Hello!
- G: Hello!
- I: What are your names?
- J: My name is Jan and this is Gosia.
- I: Where are you from?
- J: We're from Gdańsk in Poland.
- I: What are your nationalities?
- J: We're Polish.
- I: What are your jobs?
- G: I'm an Office Manager and he's a Customer Service Manager.
- I: Nice to meet you.
- J: Nice to meet you, too.
- G: Nice to meet you.

Part 3
I = Interviewer   R = Rafael
- I: Hello.
- R: Hello.
- I: What's your name?
- R: My name is Rafael.
- I: Where are you from?
- R: I'm from Brazil.
- I: What's your nationality?
- R: I'm Brazilian.
- I: What's your job?
- R: I'm a Marketing Director.
- I: Nice to meet you.
- R: Nice to meet you, too.
- I: Goodbye!
- R: Goodbye!

1.4.1   L = Liz   K = Krzystof
- L: Good morning. How may I help you?
- K: I'm here to see Yumiko Kobayashi. Sorry, I think I'm a bit early. My name is Krzysztof Grzeszak.
- L: Sorry, could you repeat that, please?
- K: It's Grzeszak. Krzysztof Grzeszak.
- L: Could you spell that, please?
- K: Grzeszak is G-R-Z-E-S-Z-A-K. Krzysztof is K-R-Z-Y-S-Z-T-O-F.
- L: OK, thanks. Hello, Yumiko. It's Liz. Mr … There's someone here to see you. … Uh-huh. … Sure. Have a seat, please. Ms Kobayashi will be ready in a few minutes.
- K: Thank you.
- L: Would you like some tea or coffee?
- K: Coffee, please. Thanks.
- L: Would you like milk or sugar?
- K: Milk, please. No sugar, thanks.
- L: Sure.

1.4.2   Y = Yumiko   K = Krzystof
- Y: Krzysztof!
- K: Hi, Yumiko.
- Y: Sorry to keep you waiting!
- K: No problem. Good to see you again!
- Y: Good to see you, too! How about a coffee?
- K: No, thanks … I already have one.
- Y: Great. So how are you?
- K: I'm really well, thanks. How about you?
- Y: I'm well, thank you. Please come in.
- K: After you.
- Y: Thanks, Krzysztof.

2.1.1   Interview 1
I = Interviewer   E = Elena
- I: People have different responsibilities at work. What's your name?
- E: My name is Elena Clarke.
- I: Where are you from?
- E: I'm from Southend-on-Sea.
- I: Where do you work?
- E: I work for an international company.
- I: What's your job?
- E: I am a Receptionist.
- I: What are your responsibilities?
- E: I answer the phone. 'Good morning, reception. How can I help?' I meet visitors and I give visitors a pass.

Interview 2
I = Interviewer   E = Ellen
- I: What's your name?
- E: My name's Ellen James.
- I: Where are you from?
- E: I'm from Leicester in England.
- I: Where do you work?
- E: I work for Small Pharma. It's a pharmaceutical company and it's in London.
- I: What's your job?
- E: I'm a Senior Research Manager.
- I: What do you do at work?
- E: I work on projects with my team and I have meetings with my manager. I make phone calls, and I write and answer emails.

Interview 3
I = Interviewer   S = Steve   A = Andrew
- I: Hello!
- S: Hello!
- I: What's your name?
- S: My name's Steve Wilson.
- I: Where are you from?
- S: I'm from London.
- I: Where do you work?
- S: I work at a big e-commerce company.
- I: What's your job?
- S: I'm a Sales Manager. I write sales reports, I manage the sales team. I have ten people in my team. I have meetings with clients. Hi! I'm Steve Wilson.
- A: Andy Morton.
- S: Hi, nice to meet you. Right this way.
- A: Let's go.
- S: I check the clients are happy.

2.4.1   A = Andrea   J = Jack
- A: Hi.
- J: Hi.
- A: You're new here, right?
- J: Yes, that's right. It's my first week.
- A: I'm Andrea. Nice to meet you.
- J: I'm Jack.
- A: Which department are you in?
- J: I work in marketing. I'm a Community Manager.
- A: Oh, really? What does a Community Manager do?
- J: Well, basically, I write blogs and provide images and videos for the website and for social media. And I check messages from customers and write answers. It's important for the company's image.
- A: I see. That sounds interesting.
- J: Erm…what about you? Where do you work?
- A: In the sales department. I'm a Sales Director.
- J: Do you travel for work?
- A: Yes, I travel a lot, especially to the north. I have meetings with my sales team and our big clients. And we go to sales conferences in Europe every year.
- J: That's interesting.
- A: Excuse me. Nice talking to you.
- J: And you! See you!

3.1.1
I = Interviewer   F = Fi
- I: Fi, Ellie and Kathryn talk about their jobs.

Part 1
- I: What's your name?
- F: My full name is Fatine Ouadaa but everyone calls me Fi.
- I: Where are you from?
- F: I'm from Morocco.
- I: What's your job?
- F: I'm a Receptionist. 'Good afternoon, Griffin Stone Moscrop & Co.'
- I: Where do you work?
- F: I work at an accountancy agency.
- I: Where are you based?
- F: We are based in Holborn, in London.
- I: When do you start work?
- F: I usually start work at two thirty.
- I: When do you finish work?
- F: I usually finish work at five thirty.
- I: What days do you work?
- F: I work Mondays, Tuesdays, Wednesdays, Thursdays and Fridays.
- I: Can you work flexible hours?
- F: I can work flexible hours. I sometimes start work at nine thirty and finish at twelve thirty.
- I: When can you take a break?
- F: I don't usually take a break because I only work for three hours.
- I: Can you speak any languages?
- F: I can speak English, French, Arabic and Spanish. 'Bonjour, avec qui je parle?' I sometimes use French, because we have French clients.
- I: When is your busy period?
- F: We're always busy in April and December.
- I: When can you go on holiday?
- F: I sometimes go on holiday in July, but I never go on holiday in December because we're very busy.

I = Interviewer   E = Ellie
- I: What's your name?
- E: My name is Ellie Wilson.
- I: Where are you from?
- E: I'm from Torquay in Devon.
- I: What's your job?
- E: I'm an Office Assistant.
- I: Where do you work?
- E: I work at a television production company.
- I: Where are you based?
- E: I'm based in central London.
- I: What days do you work?
- E: I work five days a week, Monday to Friday.
- I: When do you usually start work?
- E: I usually start work at half past nine.
- I: When do you finish work?
- E: I usually finish work at half past five.
- I: Can you work flexible hours?
- E: I can't work flexible hours. I always start at half past nine.
- I: When can you take a break?
- E: I can take a break when I want to, but I usually have lunch at one o'clock.
- I: When do you have meetings?
- E: I often have meetings in the morning. I always have meetings with my manager at twenty past ten, on Mondays.
- I: Can you speak any languages?
- E: No, I can only speak English.
- I: When is your busy period?
- E: August is usually my busy period, so I can't go on holiday then.
- I: When can you go on holiday?
- E: I usually go on holiday in September and I have a weekend break in May.

Part 2
My name's Kathryn Prattley, and I'm a Student Services Assistant at the Event Academy. I'm British and I live near Lewes, in the UK. I'm based in our head office in Lewes. We also have an office in London. I sometimes work in our London office. I work part-time, from 9.30 til 2.30. When I work in London, I work from 9.30 til 5.30. I always work five days a week, from Monday to Friday. I can work flexible hours and I can work from home if I want to. I can take a break whenever I want one – for tea or coffee – and I never have a lunch break. We always have a team meeting on Friday at 1.30. February, September and November are always busy. But summer is never busy. I have children at school, so we always go on holiday in August, in the school holidays.

123

Videoscripts

3.4.1 Y = Yumiko P = Paulo R = Rachel M = Martin

Y: OK. Thanks for coming, everyone. First thing on the agenda: Paulo, where are we with planning the new project?
P: We aren't finished. I'm sorry. The problem is people's summer holidays, but we can see the solution: we need to hire more people.
Y: OK, how many?
P: We need three extra people to work from the 1st of July to the 31st of August.
Y: Right … and with three extra people, can we meet the deadline?
P: Yes. I think we can finish by Friday the 17th of September.
Y: That's great. And Rachel, what's the situation with finding a new supplier?
R: Well, we now have three possible suppliers, but the problem is they can't make the parts we need at a good price.
Y: OK, what can we do to solve this?
R: We can look for international suppliers. They have very big factories and can make parts for less money.
Y: OK, let's do that. Can we finish on schedule?
R: No. I think we need more time. I'm sorry. Probably …the end of July, not the end of June.
Y: OK. Can we talk about this again next week?
R: Sure.
Y: And finally, Martin, can you tell us about the online invoicing system?
M: Yes. We have a problem with the website, but we can solve it. We need to change how the system works, so we need to ask an IT Specialist for help with that.
Y: Can you meet the deadline? It's the 24th of June, right?
M: Mmm…. yes, we think we can. We're on schedule.
Y: That's great. Well done everyone. Is there any other business?
All: No./No, I don't think so.

4.1.1 L = Leonora R = Rob A = Ali

L: My name is Leonora and I'm a Senior Consultant. One day, the office photocopier stopped working. I checked the paper. I turned it off and on. It didn't work. I looked at the photocopier but I didn't know what to do. I called the IT Specialist and he solved the problem.
R: My name's Rob Smith. I'm an Accountant. I had a meeting in London, and I went by metro. But the metro stopped working. My telephone stopped working, and I was on the metro with no telephone for one hour. I arrived an hour late to the meeting. The client was no longer there. I telephoned the client. I said sorry and I changed the meeting to a different day.
A: My name is Ali and I work as a Trainee Accountant. Last year, I had a difficult client. I waited a long time for the client to answer emails and send documents. I sent more and more emails but the client didn't answer, and then I saw the deadline was in two weeks. It was 17th of June and the deadline was on the 1st of July. Then I called the client, and finally he answered and sent the documents. I finished the work just before the deadline!

4.4.1 E = Emily L = Liz

E: Hello. Can I help you?
L: Hello. Do you remember me? I bought this phone yesterday, but I got home and it didn't work.
E: Really? What's the problem?
L: Well, when I make a phone call, people can't hear me.
E: Oh, no. Did you check the microphone settings?
L: Yes, I did. But it didn't work.
E: OK. And did you try turning it off and on again?
L: Yes, and restarting it, but I had the same problem.
E: Right … OK. Can I have a look at it?

4.4.2 E = Emily L = Liz

E: So, there's definitely a problem with the microphone.
L: I knew it wasn't just me.
E: No. It's definitely the phone. So, I can give you your money back, you can choose a different phone, or I can order you a new one. What would you prefer?
L: Well, I really like this model. I'd prefer a new one, please.
E: Let me just check when we can get you a replacement. I'll order it now and you can collect it on Wednesday. Is that OK?
L: Yes. That's fine.
E: OK, I'll call you when it's ready for collection. How can I contact you?
L: Well… at work. My office number is …

5.1.1 S = Sukhjinder I = Interviewer K = Keir B = Beata M = Mo R = Riaz

Part 1
S: My name is Sukhjinder. I'm an Accountant here at Accounts and Legal. Accounts and Legal is five years old. We offer accounting and legal services to small and medium companies. We have two offices, one in Brighton and this is the one in London. Twenty people work here.
I: Who are they and what are they doing?
S: Keir is the Managing Director.
K: I'm preparing a report for a client meeting this afternoon.
S: Maria is an Accountant.
M: I'm writing invoices.
S: Beata is also an Accountant.
B: I'm printing some documents.
S: Mo is an Accountant.
M: I'm writing emails and waiting for a phone call.

Part 2
S: Megan isn't here. She's visiting a client. Riaz is an Associate Director.
R: I'm making a phone call to a client. 'Hi! Can I speak to James, please?'
I: Jenny is checking invoices. And John is preparing a sales report. Everyone in the office is working very hard!

5.4.1 Conversation 1
Y = Yumiko M = Martin

Y: Hi, Martin. Do you need something?
M: Hi, Yumiko. Yes, could I ask a favour?
Y: Go on.
M: My daughter is not well and I need to pick her up from school. Could I leave early?
Y: Can you work from home?
M: Yes. I think I can.
Y: Fine. That's OK. I'll see you tomorrow. I hope your daughter feels better.
M: Thanks, Yumiko. I'm sure she will.

Conversation 2
J = Jack P = Paulo

J: Are you OK, Paulo? Can I help you?
P: Oh, yes thanks, Jack. I hurt my back at the gym. Could you put some paper in the photocopier?
J: No problem. Can I do anything else for you?
P: No, thanks. That's really nice of you.
J: Well, take it easy.
P: I will. Thanks again.

Conversation 3
A = Andrea R = Rachel

A: Hi, Rachel. Can I ask you for some help?
R: Yes, sure. I'll help if I can.
A: Well, I don't have much time to get the presentation ready for the meeting with the new clients. The deadline is Friday and I still have a lot to do. Could you help me with it?
R: I'm really sorry, Andrea, but I need to finish this report by tomorrow. I want to help, but I don't have time.
A: No. It's OK. Don't worry about it.
R: You could ask Jessica. I think she has some free time tomorrow.
A: OK. Great. I'll go and ask her. Thanks.

6.1.1 P = Presenter T = Tim E = Eleonora S = Simon

P: This is the old office of an international company. The company moved to this new office two years ago.
T: My name is Tim. I'm a Content Developer. I worked in the old office for one year. The old office was quieter and easier to work in. But the new office is lighter and more modern than the old office.
E: I'm Eleonora and I'm a Product Manager. I worked in the old office for three years. The old office was darker and more traditional than the new office. The desks were bigger. The new office is busier and noisier.
S: My name is Simon and I'm a Content Developer. I worked at the old office for three months. The new office is smaller but the facilities are better - for example, the gym and the break room. There are more meeting rooms at the new office and they're lighter.
T: I travel to work by train. The new office is further from the train station than the old office.
E: The old office was closer to the train station and it was easier for me to get to work. My journey to work is now longer.
S: I drive to work. The car park at the new office is bigger and parking is easier. My journey to work is shorter.
T: The canteen in the new office is smaller but the coffee is better. The canteen in the old office was cheaper.
E: I like the canteen in the new office but it is more expensive than the canteen in the old office.
S: The canteen in the new office is busy and noisy. But the food is really good.
T: I like the new office. I think it's better than the old office.
E: I liked the old office better.
S: I think the new office is better than the old office. I like working here.

6.4.1

Krzystof: As you can see from these bar charts, the Zindex A320 is the best laser printer-photocopier on the market and the Macinda 360 is the best inkjet printer-photocopier on the market. Ninety percent of our customers are satisfied with our products. This table shows you the three main differences between the two models. The second column is the Zindex A320 and the third column is the Macinda 360. As you can see in the second row, the Zindex is faster than the Macinda. It can print 50 pages per minute. But if you look at the third column, row three, you will see that the Macinda's guarantee is longer. Row four of the table shows the price of toner for the Zindex and ink for the Macinda. If you print 100 pages on the Zindex, you will spend one euro fifty on toner. If you print 100 pages on the Macinda, you will spend two euros on ink.
OK, so now let's look at the price, delivery time and payment terms. There is no minimum order. But if you order twenty printers, we will give you a ten percent discount on toner or ink.

7.1.1 P = Presenter B = Bernice

P: Every company has procedures. We talked to Bernice about a procedure for issuing purchase orders and paying suppliers.
B: My name is Bernice Luxford and I work as a Project Administrator for a large international company with many suppliers and contracts. I enter each contract into the system, and then I make sure that each invoice is approved for payment. This is how I do it. I receive contracts here. When I receive a new contract, I have to create a purchase order. I have to enter the supplier details: company name and address, the price and the delivery date. When I finish, the system notifies my manager, and my manager approves the purchase order. Then the system sends the purchase order number to the supplier. Then the supplier sends the invoice. The supplier has to include the purchase order number on their invoice. I check the invoice with the purchase order, and I approve it. All done!

7.4.1 Y = Yumiko   P = Paulo

Y: So, Paulo, you wanted to talk about new starters joining our company.
P: Yes. I think I know how to improve the recruitment process.
Y: Really? I didn't know we had a problem.
P: Well, there's no problem really. But I think we can make it better.
Y: OK, go on.
P: Well, as you know, HR first send a job offer to the candidate by email. If they accept the job, HR prepare a contract, and the new starter signs it.
Y: That's right. Then I ask IT to create their email address and account on the company systems. The new employee starts and their line manager gives them job-specific training. So, what do you want to change?
P: Well, why don't we use technology to make this process better?
Y: That's an interesting idea. Tell me more.
P: Can I?
Y: Sure.
P: Well, currently, someone in HR has to print two copies of the contract. And you, the Director, have to sign them. Then, an Admin Assistant sends the two copies to the candidate by post. The candidate sends one signed copy back. Then HR have to file it.
Y: I know. It can take weeks to get the contract back.

7.4.2 Y=Yumiko   P=Paulo

Y: I know. It can take weeks to get the contract back.
P: Yes, you're right. Do you remember Joe's contract? You were away for a week, on a business trip, and couldn't sign the contract. Then he was on holiday. It was a month before we got the contract.
Y: Yes, I remember. And how can we improve this? What's the solution?
P: So, why not use an electronic contracts system? We can create the contract in the system, and you can sign it.
Y: I'm not sure about that. It won't help when I'm travelling.
P: It will. It's an online system. You can sign the contract anywhere. You just need to be online, and log onto the system.
Y: Really? That sounds great.
P: It is. Candidates can also sign the contract online. Then the system saves it automatically. No paper.
Y: That's great. It's so simple. How much does it cost?
P: I'm not sure about that. There are different tools. I wanted to talk to you first about the idea.
Y: OK, could you get more information about this? And let's talk about it again next week.
P: Sure, I'll check the prices.
Y: And I think we should invite Mark from IT to that meeting.
P: That's a good idea. I'll send him an invite.

8.1.1 T = Toby   P = Presenter

T: My name is Toby Blythe and I'm Marketing Manager for Morgan Motor Company. We make handcrafted sports cars.
P: The company has five standard models, and they build fifteen cars per week.
T: The lead time for one of our cars is typically three to six months. When we receive an order for a car, the first thing we do is order the parts.
P: Morgan Motor have some parts in stock. They make some parts, and they also buy some from companies in other countries.
T: Our engines come from BMW from Germany, and from Ford from the USA. Customers can choose, for example, the colour of the interior leather, between ten and twenty different colours. We keep a number of the leather colours in stock here at the factory. Some of the more unusual colours we order in from the manufacturer. Customers can choose from around 40,000 different paint colours. To build a Morgan sports car takes around three and a half weeks. It takes a full day to make the wooden body frame. Handcrafting the body panels takes around eight hours. It takes around eight hours to paint the car. The final inspection is around four hours, and then on to its final customer. When the cars are complete, we ship around seventy percent to other countries. France and Germany, for example, are two big overseas markets. There is high demand for our cars, which gives us a waiting list of around three to six months. And the lead time can vary for our products, depending on the season and depending on the product.
P: The company launched a new car at the beginning of this year. They had a lot of orders. When demand is high, customers have to wait longer. But the car is truly special!

8.4.1 Part 1
Y = Yumiko   R = Rachel

Y: Rachel, do you have a moment?
R: Hi. Yes, I do.
Y: So, we're very happy with the project. Excellent job!
R: Oh, that's great!
Y: Yes, well done on negotiating the dates with the suppliers, and great work finding the new warehouses.
R: Thank you.
Y: This means that we can reduce the lead time by two days.
R: Wow! Great news!
Y: Absolutely. Next time, remember to ask for help if you need it!
R: Sure.
Y: And try to communicate every day with the team.
R: Mmm, yes.
Y: But, well done!

Part 2
Y = Yumiko   A = Andrea

Y: Andrea, I just want to say – great work on Thursday!
A: Oh, thanks, Yumiko.
Y: It was a fantastic presentation. Great job selling the product to our clients. And good work answering all those questions.
A: Thanks.
Y: The result is that the clients are now very interested. So in future, invite more people!
A: Sure.
Y: And remember to show the clients our customer reviews.
A: Of course.
Y: Well done.

Audioscripts

1.01
1 Lena, this is Jorge. He's from Spain.
2 I'm Kathy. I'm Irish.
3 Excuse me. Are you Miss Sato?

1.02
A
A: I'm Kathy. I'm Irish.
B: Nice to meet you.
B
A: Excuse me. Are you Miss Sato?
B: Yes, I am.
C
A: Lena, this is Jorge. He's from Spain.
B: Hi, I'm Lena. I'm from Germany.

1.03
1
Mi = Miguel   Ma = Marcin   P = Paola
Mi: Marcin, this is Paola. She's Brazilian.
Ma: Hi, Paola. Nice to meet you.
P: Nice to meet you, too. Where are you from, Marcin?
Ma: I'm Polish.
P: Are you from Warsaw?
Ma: No, I'm not. I'm from Krakow.
P: And are you from Mexico, Miguel?
Mi: Yes, that's right.
2
Su = Suresh   Sh = Shoko
Su: Are you Japanese, Shoko?
Sh: Yes, I am. I'm from Tokyo. And you?
Su: I'm from India.
Sh: And where is Paola from?
Su: She's from Brazil.

1.04
Argentina	Argentinian
China	Chinese
Brazil	Brazilian
Germany	German
India	Indian
Ireland	Irish
Japan	Japanese
Mexico	Mexican
Poland	Polish
Spain	Spanish
the UK	British
the USA	American

1.05 H = Hans   Ma = Maria   Mi = Mike   L = Lisa
H: Hello, I'm Hans.
Ma: Hi, Hans. My name's Maria.
H: Nice to meet you.
Ma: Nice to meet you, too.
H: Are you from Argentina?
Ma: No, I'm not. I'm Brazilian.
H: Is your boss Brazilian?
Ma: No, she isn't. She's from Mexico.
Mi: Maria! Hello!
Ma: Hi, Mike! And Lisa! Hans, this is Mike and Lisa. They are from the UK.
H: Nice to meet you.
Mi/L: Nice to meet you, Hans. / Hi!
H: Are you from London?
L: No, we aren't. We are from Liverpool.

1.06 L = Leah   J = Jacek
L: What's your address, Jacek?
J: It's 28 Oak Road, London, W55 1TF.
L: What's your ID card number?
J: It's 124232.
L: What's your email address?
J: It's j.iwaniec@ccce.com. All lower case.
L: OK, thanks. And what's your phone number?
J: It's 020 7946 0800.

1.07
My email address is W underscore Schmidt at net hyphen mail dot com. That's capital W, underscore, capital S, lowercase c-h-m-i-d-t, at all lower case net hyphen mail dot com.

1.08
1
A: What's your email address?
B: It's all lower case. Ben at abc dot net. That's b-e-n at abc dot net.
2
A: What's your email address?
B: It's all capitals. Jan dot Smith at Smith dot com. J-A-N dot S-M-I-T-H at S-M-I-T-H dot com.
3
A: What's your email address?
B: Capital U, lower case w-e at one hyphen two hyphen three dot p-l.
4
A: What's your email address?
B: It's Alex underscore Aziz at jump dot j-p. That's capital A, lower case l-e-x, underscore, capital A, lower case z-i-z at all lower case j-u-m-p dot jp.
5
A: What's your email address?
B: It's all lower case, s-z-u-l-g-i-t hyphen k at b-i-g-i-o dot org.

1.09
A: I just need to take a few details …
B: OK, that's fine.
A: What's your surname?
B: It's Weber.
A: Can you spell that, please?
B: Sure. It's W-E-B-E-R.
A: Weber. OK, got it. You're … Anna Weber?
B: Yes, that's right.
A: Your gender is female …
B: Right …
A: What's your nationality?
B: My nationality? I'm German.
A: Sorry, could you repeat that, please?
B: I'm German – I'm from Germany.
A: OK, got it. Thanks. And your marital status?
B: Sorry?
A: Marital status? Are you married or single?
B: I'm married.
A: Married. OK, thanks. And your email?
B: Sorry?
A: What's your email address?
B: It's all lower case, a underscore weber at net hyphen mail dot d-e.
A: All lower case, a underscore weber at net hyphen mail dot d-e.
B: Yes, right.
A: What's your phone number?
B: Two three two, one oh five six.
A: Two three two, one oh five six.
B: Right.
A: OK. What's your emergency contact number?
B: Let's see … . That's Hans Weber. Four five seven, double-eight one two.
A: Four five seven, double-eight one two? OK, got it. And finally, what's your ID card number?
B: My ID card number?
A: Or your passport number. Can you give me that, please?
B: Sure. My ID card number is T one three two, four seven nine double-oh.
A: T one three two …
B: T one three two, four seven nine double-oh.
A: OK, thank you.

1.10
1
My company has three locations in three countries. I work at the head office in Munich, Germany. I work for the sales department. There are five people in my department. The office is large and modern. It's very light. There is a small canteen, but unfortunately, there is no gym.
2
I work in the factory in China, in the manufacturing division. The factory is modern, but it's also noisy. I work in the production department. There's a canteen. And there's an employee break room. The break room is quiet!
3
I work in the warehouse in Warsaw. It's old-fashioned – and dark. But it's OK. I'm the manager of the distribution division. There are no offices here. In the warehouse, there's a storage area and a shipping and receiving department. There is no canteen, but there are small restaurants near the warehouse.

2.01
1 Qatar Airways provides air transport services.
2 Allianz provides financial services.
3 Volkswagen designs, makes and sells cars.
4 Amazon sells books and other products online.
5 Inditex makes and sells clothes in shops and online.
6 Samsung makes mobile phones and home electronics.

2.02
a hundred
one hundred
three hundred and twenty
six hundred and forty-seven
a thousand
one thousand
fifty-five thousand, three hundred and sixty-seven
seventy-eight thousand, one hundred and thirteen
a hundred thousand
one hundred thousand
three hundred and sixty thousand
eight hundred and ninety-two thousand, six hundred and seventeen
a million
one million

2.03
Allianz has over 140,00 employees in more than seventy countries.
Amazon has over 100,000 warehouse robots.
Qatar Airways has 220 aircraft and flies to over 150 destinations.
Inditex has over 7,000 stores and over 174,000 employees in ninety-six countries.

2.04
We are an international transport company. We provide global logistics services. Our global head office is based in Bonn, Germany. We have over 360 offices in 220 countries. We have 85,000 staff and 250 aircraft.

2.05
Monday, Tuesday, Wednesday, Thursday, Friday, Saturday, Sunday

2.06 P = Patricia   A = Anthony   K = Katia
P: Hello, my name's Patricia Williams.
A: Nice to meet you! I'm Anthony Kowalski.
P: Kowalski. Where are you from, Anthony? Are you Polish?
A: No, I'm from Birmingham in England but I'm based in Germany. What about you? You're American, right?
P: Yes, that's right. I'm from Seattle.
A: Ah! Seattle! A great city!
P: Yeah, it is! I live and work in London now. What do you do, Anthony?
A: I work in digital marketing. I'm a Social Media Manager.
P: It's all digital marketing today, isn't it?
A: Yes, you're right!
P: What do you do at work?
A: I write blogs and make videos and content for our website and social media. And I answer guests' messages. Communication with guests is an important part of my job.
P: Really? What does your company do?
A: It's a hotel group. We have over 200 hotels in eighteen countries. In fact, this is one of our hotels.
P: Really! It's a nice hotel, light and modern. I like it.

Audioscripts

And there's a large gym.
Yeah, but I don't have time for the gym!
What about you, erm ... Sorry, what's your name again?
Patricia ... Patricia Williams.
Yeah, sorry, Patricia, what do you do?
I'm a Digital Project Manager.
And what does a Digital Project Manager do?
Well, my company provides design services to small businesses. We work on websites, mobile apps, social media and software. I have meetings with clients and manage a team of designers.
That sounds interesting! Do you travel for work?
Yes! We have projects all over the country. I like my job but travel is boring.
Oh, I see. I don't travel for work and I work at home on Fridays.
That sounds good!
Hi, Anthony.
Ah! Hello Katia! Katia, this is Patricia. She's a Digital Project Manager. Katia is a Marketing Assistant in my department.
Nice to meet you!
Nice to meet you, too!
Anthony, I have a message from Mike. There's a problem.
OK! Thanks! Excuse us, Patricia. Nice talking to you.
And you!

2.07
1 Where are you from, Anthony?
2 What about you? You're American, right?
3 What do you do, Anthony?
4 What do you do at work?
5 What does your company do?
6 Sorry, what's your name again?
7 Patricia, what do you do?
8 What does a Digital Project Manager do?
9 Do you travel for work?

3.01
January, February, March, April, May, June, July, August, September, October, November, December

3.02
Emily: Summer is always quiet in my job so I usually go on holiday in January or February. We often get busy in autumn so I can't take much time off in March or April but I can usually take two or three days. Winter is a very busy period so I can't go on holiday in July or August. Spring is not very busy, so I always take two weeks in September or October. This September I want to go to Japan. I can speak Japanese and I love Japanese culture so ...
Mark: The end of the year is always busy so I can't go on holiday in November or December. I often go on holiday after New Year, usually in early January. March, April and May are also busy so I can never take time off in spring. We're not very busy in summer and autumn so I can go on holiday from June to October. I usually go on holiday for two weeks in June or July. I can't speak other languages, so we usually stay in our country. We don't ...

3.03
In the new flexi-time system, staff need to work thirty-seven hours a week. They can choose when they start and finish work and they can decide when to go to lunch. All employees need to be in the office from 10.30 a.m. to 3 p.m. This means employees can't start after 10.30 a.m. They can't finish work before 3 p.m. The building opens at 7 a.m. so employees can start work then. Employees can take one hour for lunch from 11.15 a.m. to 2.45 p.m. They can't take lunch before 11.15 a.m. or after 2.45 p.m. They can work until 8 p.m. when the building closes. Remember, if you drive to work, you can only park your car in spaces 120–225. Employees need their ID card or they can't enter the car park.

3.04
1 ten o'clock
2 ten p.m.
3 twelve
4 seven thirty
5 quarter past three
6 eleven forty-five
7 ten past eight
8 four forty

3.05
So in 15th place is car manufacturer Toyota Motor Corporation from Japan with a value of 238.9 billion dollars - the only Japanese company on this list. Then, in 14th place, it's the Swiss company Nestlé, and in 13th place is the American company General Electric. In 12th place, another American company, Wal-Mart Stores, and then in 11th place it's telecommunications company China Mobile, from Hong Kong.
And so, to the top ten!
Another company from Switzerland is in 10th place – Novartis, the pharmaceutical company – with a value of 267.8 billion dollars. Then in 9th place, one of two Chinese companies in the top ten – the Industrial and Commercial Bank of China. In 8th place is Johnson and Johnson from the USA. Another financial services company is in 7th place, Wells Fargo, also from the USA. And the second Chinese company in the top ten is PetroChina, in 6th place with a value of 329.7 billion dollars.
And now to the 'big five', and they are all from the USA this year.
In 5th place, with a value of 333.5 billion dollars, is Microsoft.
In 4th place, with a value of 345.8 billion dollars, is Google.
And in 3rd place, it's financial services company Berkshire Hathaway.
In 2nd place this year we have ExxonMobil, with a value of 356.5 billion dollars.
And this year's winner, in 1st place – a very, very famous brand in consumer electronics and IT – it's Apple with a value of 724.7 billion dollars.

3.06
1 Our department always has a meeting on the 1st Thursday of the month.
2 Mr Barker's office is on the 32nd floor.
3 The delivery arrives on the 10th of November.
4 Can you come to Sam's 30th birthday on Monday?
5 That's the 15th email today.
6 My holiday starts on the 9th of July.
7 Thank you for waiting, you are 5th in line.
8 I'm out of the office from the 20th of January for a week.

3.07
1 The fourteenth of September twenty twenty one.
2 The eleventh of April twenty eighteen.
3 The twenty first of November twenty twenty.
4 The third of June nineteen ninety two.
5 The thirteenth of December twenty nineteen.
6 The twenty second of March twenty twenty one.
7 The thirtieth of July two thousand and six.

3.08
I always win 1st prize.
They have a business trip on the 10th of August.
I live on the 16th floor.
It's her 90th birthday tomorrow.
He wants to meet you on the 15th January.
You're the 50th customer today.
Can you come to a party on Tuesday? It's Mark's 60th birthday.
She works on 19th street.
I'm going on holiday on the 30th of July.
My birthday is on the 13th of July.

3.09 M = Michaela C = Colin
M: Good afternoon. Michaela Werner speaking. How can I help you?
C: Hi Michaela, it's Colin.
M: Hi, Colin. How are you?
C: I'm good, thanks. So, you have a new house – are you happy?
M: Yes, I am. Really happy. And can I take some time off? I really need four or five days.
C: Yes, of course you can but I'm afraid you can't take all the days you want. Bill, Conor and I all have holidays in July. Connor from the 11th to the 22nd of July and Bill from the 11th to the 15th of July. Then I go on holiday on the 21st of July. And we can't have three people off at the same time!
M: OK. I understand.
C: So you can take from Monday the 18th to Wednesday the 20th when Bill is back from his holiday and before I go on my holiday. Does that work? I know it's not perfect but that's what I can offer.
M: That's not great but OK. I'll take those three days.
C: OK. Can you finish the sales report before you go?
M: No problem. I can finish it by Friday the 15th of July.
C: Thank you! See you later!
M: Yes. Thanks, Colin. Bye.
C: Bye, Michaela.

4.01
1 The headphones stopped working. I saw the people talking but there was no sound.
2 I sent the report after the deadline. The project was delayed.
3 We had a meeting at 3 p.m. yesterday. Tom was late, but he said sorry when he arrived.
4 I wrote the wrong address last week. I went to the wrong office this morning.
5 I made a mistake on an invoice. The client complained and we gave him the money back.

4.02 M = Maria S = Sandra
M: Good Morning. Meyer & McNulty. How can I help you?
S: Hello, could I speak to Chris, please?
M: I'm afraid Chris is in a meeting at the moment. Can I take a message?
S: Yes please. This is Sandra Dennison from ATQ Global. We just got an invoice for our last order.
M: OK.
S: And it looks like some of the information is wrong.
M: Oh no. I'm sorry about that. What's the problem?
S: I think one of the items we ordered wasn't included. Could you ask Chris to call me to check it?
M: OK, does he have your phone number?
S: I think so but I'll give it to you now. It's 45 895 3421.
M: So that's 45 895 3421. Is that right?
S: That's right
M: OK. I'll give Chris the message. Can I help you with anything else?
S: No, thanks. Bye.
M: Bye.

4.03
1 How can I help you?
2 Could I speak to Chris, please?
3 I'm afraid Chris is in a meeting.
4 Can I take a message?
5 This is Sandra Dennison from ATQ Global.
6 I'm sorry about that.
7 Could you ask Chris to call me?
8 Is that right?
9 I'll give Chris the message.
10 Can I help you with anything else?

Audioscripts

4.04 S = Sandra C = Chris
S: Good Morning, ATQ Global. Can I help you?
C: Hi, this is Chris from Meyer & McNulty. Can I speak to Sandra, please?
S: Hi, Chris. This is Sandra.
C: Hi, Sandra. I'm returning your call. Is there a problem with your invoice?
S: That's right. There's some information missing.
C: Really? What's missing?
S: Well, we ordered black ink and colour ink but the invoice only shows the black.
C: OK. I can check what you ordered on the database. Just a minute.
S: No problem.
C: Hello, Sandra?
S: Hi.
C: So I'm afraid we only have a record of the black ink. I can add the colour ink to your order now.
S: OK.
C: So you want 200 black ink and 50 colour ink. Is that right?
S: That's right.
C: So, I can add this to your order and I'll create a new invoice. I'll send you a copy of the new invoice today.
S: OK. Thanks, Chris. Will this delay the delivery?
C: No. I can ask the team to add it to your order and we'll send it tomorrow.
S: OK. Great.
C: Can I help you with anything else?
S: No, that's it. Bye.
C: Bye.

4.05
1 Hi, Chris. This is Sandra.
2 Hi, Sandra. I'm returning your call.
3 So I'm afraid we only have a record of the black ink.
4 I can add the colour ink to your order now.
5 I'll create a new invoice.
6 I'll send you a copy of the new invoice today.
7 No. I can ask the team to add it to your order.
8 Can I help you with anything else?

4.06
1
A: Sorry, this is too much. I only bought three. This is the price for four.
B: I'm very sorry about that. I'll just change it and print you a new one.
2
A: When I make a video call, people can't hear me.
B: Really? Did you check the microphone settings?
3
A: I bought this yesterday but when I took it out of the box, I saw the screen was damaged.
B: I'm very sorry. Can I have a look at it?

5.01
Jane: As a Sales Manager, I go to a lot of meetings. I have seven or eight meetings a week. I normally visit clients three or four times a week, so I have a meeting first to prepare for the visits and then I go to the meetings with the clients.
Katie: I'm an HR Manager for a large company. Because we have over twenty offices, my job is all about email. I send about fifty a day and read hundreds. I also make a lot of phone calls, probably twenty or thirty a day. The good thing is I talk to a lot of people and I like that.
Mark: I work in purchasing. I visit suppliers in my job. After each visit, I write a report about the supplier. In my report I explain if they meet our product specifications. I visit three or four suppliers a month and write a report for each one.

5.02
1
A: Can we arrange a meeting with the client next week?
B: Sure. I'm free on Wednesday.
2
A: Did you talk to Chris?
B: No, I didn't. I need to speak to him tomorrow.
3
A: What did you talk about in the meeting?
B: We checked the product specifications.
4
A: Sorry, but I need to cancel the meeting today.
B: OK. I'll email Sandra and tell her.
5
A: How many different models do you have?
B: We have twenty-five models in our product range.
6
A: Can we postpone the meeting until next week?
B: Yes. Can we have it on Monday?
7
A: What is the best thing about your products?
B: We have very high product quality.
8
A: Do you know the date of the product launch?
B: I think it's the 22nd of May.

5.03
1
P = Paulo Gonzalez B = Bill Smith
P: Good morning. Production. Paulo Gonzalez speaking.
B: Hi, Paulo. It's Bill.
P: Hi, Bill. How are you?
B: Good thanks. Listen, we have the specifications for the new product ready. Can we arrange a meeting to talk about them?
P: That's great news. Yes. I can do this afternoon.
B: Oh, I can't do this afternoon. I have a meeting with a supplier. Are you free tomorrow morning?
P: Let me just check. Yes, I'm free from 9 to 10.30.
B: That's great. Let's meet then. I'll come to your office.
P: Great. See you then. Bye.
B: Bye.
2
S = Sandra Morelo B = Bill Smith
S: Good afternoon. P.B. Turner. How can I help you?
B: Hello, could I speak to Sandra Morelo, please?
S: Speaking.
B: Hello, Sandra, this is Bill from JTSQ manufacturing.
S: Oh, hello.
B: You sent us an email asking for information about our product range.
S: That's right.
B: I'm calling to arrange a meeting. I'd like to visit you and talk about our range. We could also talk about your needs. Are you free on the 18th?
S: Let me just check. Yes, I'm free on Monday the 18th at 2 p.m. Does that work for you?
B: Yes, I'm available then. I'll see you on the 18th.
S: I'll look forward to it. Bye.
B: Bye.
3
B = Bill Smith N = Noriko Yoshiwa
B: Hello. JTSQ Manufacturing.
N: Good morning. Could I speak to Bill Smith, please?
B: This is Bill.
N: Hello, Bill. It's Noriko Yoshiwa at Moti Nero here.
B: Hello, Noriko. How are you?
N: I'm good thanks. Listen. I'm afraid I need to postpone our meeting on the 15th to talk about our supply reorder. I have another appointment and I can't come to the meeting.
B: OK, that's not a problem. I'm free in the morning on Monday the 18th.
N: Oh no, I'm not available on the 18th. Are you free on the 19th?
B: I'm available in the morning but I'm busy in the afternoon.
N: OK. Can we do 9 to 11 a.m. on the 19th?
B: Yes, that's fine. I'll see you then.
N: Great. Thanks. Bye.
B: Bye.

5.04
A: Hello. Travelli. Marco Travelli speaking.
B: Hi, Marco. This is Dianne Grant at Malladi Tech here.
A: Hello, Dianne. How are you?
B: I'm good, thanks. Listen, we have a new product range. Can we arrange a meeting to talk about it?
A: Yes. That would be great.
B: Great. Are you free on Monday?
A: Let me just check. Sorry, I'm busy on Monday. I'm free on Tuesday morning.
B: Oh. I can't do Tuesday. Can we do Wednesday morning?
A: Yes, that's fine. I'll see you then.
B: Great, see you on Wednesday. Bye.
A: Bye.

5.05
Conversation 1
A: Sorry, Paul, can I ask a favour?
B: Sure, Tony. How can I help?
A: I can't find the presentation we're working on. Where did you save it?
B: Oh ... it's in the 'product descriptions' folder.
A: OK. Found it. Thanks.
Conversation 2
A: Monika, do you have a minute?
B: Yes, sure. How can I help?
A: I'm looking for Viktor Dorret's contact details. Do you have them?
B: Just a minute. Here they are. I'll email them to you.
A: OK, thanks.

5.06 Y = Yumiko M = Martin
Y: Hi, Martin. Do you need something?
M: Hi, Yumiko. Yes, could I ask a favour?
Y: Go on.
M: My daughter is not well and I need to pick her up from school. Could I leave early?
Y: Can you work from home?
M: Yes. I think I can.
Y: Fine. That's OK. I'll see you tomorrow. I hope your daughter feels better.
M: Thanks, Yumiko. I'm sure she will.

6.01
Now, let's look at our office costs. This bar chart shows the main differences in costs between the old office and the new office. As you can see, the rent of the new office is cheaper by £8,000. If you look at the cost of electricity, water, etc., you'll see that this cost is also lower. The cost of office supplies, for example paper, ink, pens and phones is the same, but we pay a little less for the internet. So in total we save about 15 percent per month on our new office.

6.02
Anna: So, we think 23 Beaker Street is the best option. This slide shows a list of details about 23 Beaker Street. It's bigger than our office now, and it's close to the city centre. It's also close to a train station and a bus stop. They're about a five-minute walk.
However, as you can see, it's not perfect because the car park is smaller and the internet is slower than what we have at the moment.
Tony: Now, let's look at prices. The office costs $1,900 a month so it's more expensive than our office at the moment but cheaper than other offices in the city centre. If you look at the final bullet point, you will see that we can choose a five- or ten-year contract, so that's really good.

7.01
A: So, to issue a purchase order, you have to go into the payment system. First, you have to open the system.
B: OK.

Audioscripts

A: Then you enter the supplier's details: name, address, etc. on the system.
B: Do I have to do that every time?
A: No, you don't. You can choose it from a list here. When you have the supplier's details, you enter the price here and the delivery date here. You can find the information on the contract.
B: And do I notify the supplier that the purchase order's ready?
A: No, you don't have to do that. The system notifies the supplier automatically by email.
B: OK, that's clear. What's next?
A: The supplier delivers the items and requests payment.
B: So they have to tell us to pay them. Right?
A: Yes, they issue an invoice with the purchase order number on it. We can't pay invoices without a purchase order number. You have to check the invoice against the purchase order. If it's correct, you can request management approval. The manager approves the payment. And when they approve it, you can make the payment. but that's later. Do you want to try to create a purchase order?
B: Yes, please.

7.02
A: So we have a problem. We're receiving lots of complaints about late deliveries, missing items and incorrect invoices.
B: I know but I don't understand why. We're also receiving lots of positive comments about deliveries and orders.
A: Right. So, I think we have a problem in the workflow. When we receive an order in the sales department, we always check the inventory system and, if we have enough items, we give a delivery date and send the invoice to the customer.
B: Yes, but often when my warehouse team go to collect the items, we can't always find all of them. Sometimes the inventory system doesn't have the correct data.
A: So that's the problem. When you don't have all the items, what do you do?
B: Well, we wait for more items to arrive or we send the items we have. If we only send the items we have, then we have to send the other items later.
A: OK. So now we know why orders are late and why people don't always get all the items they ordered. But why is this happening?
B: Well, the problems with delivery only happen with large orders. Usually fifty items or more. Do you check with the warehouse before you approve the order?
A: No, we just take the number from the system.
B: Ah ... but the system only updates on Thursdays.
A: So I think that's the answer. If the system only updates once a week then my sales team are looking at old information.
B: OK. And when we look in the warehouse, we don't have the right number of items.
A: Exactly, so we could ...

7.03
So I received a job offer after the interview and I accepted. Then the company sent me a contract. I signed it and sent it back with my medical certificate and qualifications. On the first day, I had a tour of the office and met my colleagues. I had an induction meeting and did health and safety training. The company managed everything well. The only problem was I didn't receive job-specific training for three months. I had to ask my colleagues what to do.

8.01
So, let's look at the MX2 standard model in the database. Ah yes, here it is. Cortadino MX 2, standard model.
Now, there is high demand for this model at the moment and we can see here that it's out of stock. We need to order it from the factory. For the MX 2, manufacturing happens in Asia and takes five working days. Then, shipping from Asia is six and a half weeks. Finally, when we receive it, we always need one to two working days for final inspection. So the lead time is eight weeks. Any questions?

8.02   P = Paul   J = Julia
P: Right, Julia – your turn! Find the Cortadino N20 in the database.
J: OK, sure. Is this it?
P: Yes. So, what can you tell me about the N20?
J: Um ...OK ... the N20 is in stock. So we don't need to order it from the factory – there are fifty models in the Liège warehouse.
P: Good ...
J: And shipping from Liège is five to six working days. And final inspection takes one to two days. So the lead time is ... six to eight working days?
P: Yes! Well done.

R2.01
1   a hundred and seventy, one hundred and seventy
2   five hundred and twenty-five
3   eight hundred and fifteen
4   two thousand and thirty-six
5   forty-four thousand, two hundred and eight
6   sixty-three thousand, nine hundred and eighteen
7   a hundred thousand, one hundred thousand
8   three hundred and twenty-one thousand
9   seven hundred and fifty-two thousand, four hundred
10   a million, one million

R3.01
1   the 23rd of November twenty fifteen
2   the 14th of May two thousand and four
3   the 22nd of March twenty twenty-three
4   the 4th of April eighteen ninety-nine
5   the 3rd of December nineteen seventy-three
6   the 24th of February nineteen sixty-five
7   the 18th of August twenty thirteen
8   the 30th of September twenty forty

R3.02
1   The meeting is at half past eleven.
2   He starts work at eight forty-five.
3   I usually finish work at five thirty.
4   We have lunch at two o'clock.
5   The building closes at quarter to eight.
6   The deadline is at half past six.

P1.02
A, B, C, D, E, F, G, H, I, J, K, L, M, N, O, P, Q, R, S, T, U, V, W, X, Y, Z

P1.03
1   DHL
2   KFC
3   BMW
4   LG
5   IBM
6   KLM
7   CNN
8   UPS
9   HSBC
10   MTV

P1.04
1   It's Ms Marquez. That's M-A-R-Q-U-E-Z.
2   Their email address is all capitals I-N-F-O at all lower case b-l-k-n dot com.
3   Her surname is Nowak-Tkacz. That's N-O-W-A-K hyphen T-K-A-C-Z.
4   My address is lower case j-j underscore lower case d-i-a-z at lower case h-o-l-a dot m-x.
5   The address is all lower case w-w-w dot u-o-q dot j-p.
6   It's office at capital I lower case n-t-e-r hyphen all capital F-T-V dot a-r.

P1.08
/s/ breaks nights
/z/ jobs locations
/ɪz/ buses warehouses

P2.02
1   thirty invoices
2   thirteen projects
3   forty thousand euros
4   fifteen products
5   sixty employees
6   seventy customers
7   eighteen million dollars
8   ninety cars

P2.04
1   three hundred and fourteen
2   nine hundred and seventy-seven
3   eight thousand, two hundred and thirty-nine
4   thirty-three thousand, four hundred and fourteen
5   four hundred and thirty-two thousand, seven hundred and forty-six
6   seven million, nine hundred and fifty thousand, one hundred and ten
7   thirteen million, eight hundred thousand, five hundred and fourteen
8   four hundred and twenty-three million, forty nine thousand, one hundred and thirteen

P3.08
1   The fourteenth of August two thousand and five.
2   It's on the fortieth floor.
3   The eleventh of November nineteen eighteen.
4   It's his thirtieth birthday.
5   It's their fifteenth shop in the UK.
6   The thirteenth of June twenty fourteen.
7   It's their seventeenth order.
8   The twenty-third of November twenty nineteen.

P4.04
1   They arrive on time.
2   I managed a big team.
3   We fixed problems.
4   They accepted my offers.
5   We talk about the budget.
6   I attended all the meetings.

P8.03
month, money, colour, love, other, company

P8.06
word, work, world, worse, worst

Vocabulary list

Key vocabulary

Unit 1

1.1
- Argentina
- Brazil
- China
- Germany
- India
- Ireland
- Japan
- Mexico
- Poland
- Spain
- The UK
- The USA

- American
- Argentinian
- Brazilian
- British
- Chinese
- German
- Indian
- Irish
- Japanese
- Mexican
- Polish
- Spanish

1.2
- address (*noun*)
- email address
- emergency contact number
- first name / given name
- gender (*noun*)
- home address
- ID card [number]
- marital status
- middle name
- nationality
- passport [number]
- phone/mobile/cell number
- postcode / zip code
- surname / last name
- title (*noun*)

- at (@)
- capital
- dot (*noun*)
- hyphen (*noun*)
- lower case
- underscore (*noun*)

1.3
- building
- canteen
- employee break room
- facilities
- factory
- gym
- office
- warehouse (*noun*)

- department
- distribution
- division
- manufacturing
- production
- sales
- shipping and receiving

- dark
- large
- light
- modern
- noisy
- old-fashioned
- quiet
- small

1.4
- coffee
- milk
- sugar
- tea
- water (*noun*)

- coffee machine
- laptop
- photocopier
- printer
- tablet
- whiteboard

Unit 2

2.1
- Digital Designer
- IT Specialist
- Production Engineer
- Sales Manager

- answer (*verb*)
- check (*verb*)
- have
- make
- manage
- sell

Vocabulary list

work (*verb*) _____
write _____

2.2
car _____
e-reader _____
laptop/computer _____
mobile phone _____
TV _____
washing machine _____

design cars _____
make clothes _____
make consumer electronics _____
provide air transport services _____
provide financial services _____
sell products online _____

2.3
Monday _____
Tuesday _____
Wednesday _____
Thursday _____
Friday _____
Saturday _____
Sunday _____

2.4
family _____
free-time activities _____
health _____
home town _____
job _____
nationality _____
nothing _____
weather (*noun*) _____
work (*noun*) _____

boring _____
good _____
great _____
interesting _____

Unit 3

3.1
autumn _____
spring _____
summer _____
winter _____

January _____
February _____
March _____
April _____
May _____
June _____
July _____
August _____
September _____
October _____
November _____
December _____

3.3
broken _____
damaged _____
incorrect _____
late _____
missing _____

3.4
planning meeting _____
problem-solving meeting _____
progress meeting _____

Unit 4

4.1
give _____
go _____
have _____
make _____
say _____
see _____
send _____
write _____

4.2
ask for _____
ask to _____
check _____
check that _____
contact about _____
contact by _____
send _____
send to _____

never _____
once or twice a month _____
a few times a week _____
sometimes _____
every day _____
all the time _____

Vocabulary list

Unit 5

5.1
go to a meeting
have a meeting
prepare for a meeting

make a phone call
receive a phone call
wait for a phone call

write a report
write an email
write minutes

visit a client
visit a colleague
visit a supplier

5.2
product launch
product quality
product range
product specifications

arrange a meeting
cancel a meeting
postpone a meeting

5.3
agenda
contract (noun)
document (noun)
invoice (noun)
meeting minutes
notes
presentation slides
report (noun)
spreadsheet

Unit 6

6.1
bad
big
busy
cheap
close (adjective)
difficult
easy
expensive
far
good
long

short
spacious
traditional

6.2
delivery time
minimum order
payment terms
product name
total price
unit price

6.3
competitive price
fixed-term contract
free national and international calls
unlimited data/texts
wide range

6.4
bar chart
bullet point
column
diagram (noun)
line graph
list (noun)
pie chart
row (noun)
table (noun)

Unit 7

7.1
approve
enter
issue (verb)
notify
request (verb)
supply (verb)

invoice (noun)
purchase order

7.2
envelope
headphones
paper
pen (noun)
pencil (noun)
printer ink cartridge
ring binder
stapler

Vocabulary list

clear (*adjective*) _____
complicated _____
efficient _____
excellent _____
poor _____
reliable _____
simple _____
unreliable _____

7.3
check (*verb*) _____
click (*verb*) _____
complete _____
confirm _____
download (*verb*) _____
forget _____
organise _____
phone (*verb*) _____
prepare _____
receive _____
remember _____
send _____

7.4
bank details _____
diploma _____
health and safety training _____
induction meeting _____
job-specific training _____
medical certificate _____
office tour _____
qualification _____
reference (*noun*) _____

Unit 8

8.1
customer _____
factory _____
materials _____
shipping _____
shop (*noun*) _____
warehouse (*noun*) _____

custom model _____
demand (*noun*) _____
in stock _____
inspection _____
lead time _____
manufacturing _____
out of stock _____
standard model _____

8.2
automate tasks _____
negotiate _____
outsource work _____
relocate _____
review expenses _____
save energy _____
upgrade technology _____
work remotely _____

clothes _____
food _____
free-time activities _____
mortgage (*noun*) _____
rent (*noun*) _____
transport (*noun*) _____

8.3
architect (*noun*) _____
chef _____
fashion designer _____
teacher _____

design student tests _____
design summer/winter collections _____
order food supplies _____
plan building size _____
plan lessons _____
plan menus _____
plan fashion shows _____
prepare floor plans _____

Notes

Notes